Dundrum, Stillorgan and Rathfarnham

Gateway to the Mountains

Paintings by Olivia Hayes

Text by Christopher Ryan

Cottage
Publications

First published by Cottage Publications,
an imprint of Laurel Cottage Ltd.
Donaghadee, N. Ireland 2002.
Copyrights Reserved.
© Illustrations by Olivia Hayes 2002.
© Text by Christopher Ryan 2002.
All rights reserved.
No part of this book may be reproduced or stored
on any media without the express written
permission of the publishers.
Design & origination in Northern Ireland.
Printed & bound in Singapore.

ISBN 1 900935 27 9

Olivia Hayes

Olivia Hayes was born in Dublin and has lived most of her life in the Dundrum-Rathfarnham area. She is a graduate of the National College of Art and Design and has obtained a post-graduate degree in Art Education. Working as a professional artist since 1981, she exhibits regularly in several Dublin galleries and as a guest artist for a number of Dublin art groups. She is involved in adult art-education in South Dublin and Northern Wicklow. She has had two sell-out one-woman shows in Dublin and is a committee member of the Dublin Painting and Sketching Club.

Olivia is a keen hillwalker in the Dublin and Wicklow mountains, which have provided a source of inspiration to her painting for many years.

Christopher Ryan

Christopher Ryan, born in east Co. Limerick, graduated at UCD: he taught student nurses at St. John of God Hospital, Stillorgan, for thirty years from which he took early retirement.

His interests include local history which he studied at Maynooth, and genealogy to which he devotes much time. He set up the 'Ballinteer Family History Society' in 1993 and is editor of the Society's journal *'Gateway to the Past'*.

He compiled *'Lewis' Dublin'*, edited *'Aspects of Irish Genealogy 3'*, and was author of *'Simpson's Hospital'* and *'The Parish of St John the Evangelist, Ballinteer'*. He is also a regular contributor to genealogical journals.

Christopher lives in Ballinteer with his wife Lily.

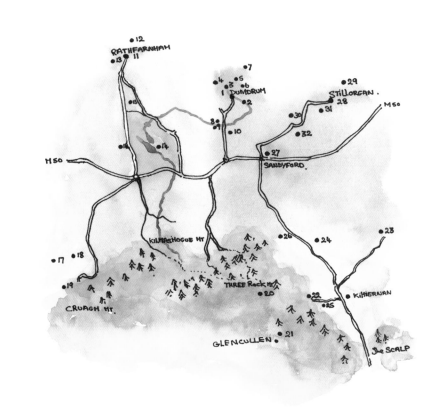

Contents

South Dublin, From Landscape to People

"I lived on a hill top with the most beautiful view in the World: I had only to open my eyes to see such pictures as no painter could paint for me".

These were the words of George Bernard Shaw as he attempted to describe the overwhelming beauty of the landscape of south-east County Dublin when he lived at Dalkey.

The geological events which shaped County Dublin span a period of just over 250 million years from what the geologists call the Cambrian to the lower Carboniferous periods. As the environment changed through this almost unimaginable length of time, marine conditions gave way to periods of volcanic activity and deep underground a mass of molten rock rose up to form a broad elongated dome running in a south-westerly direction. The rock slowly cooled to form the greatest mass of granite in the British Isles, a formation which was gradually exposed as the overlying layers of rock were worn away by the inexorable effects of wind, water and ice. This huge Leinster Granite, which forms the bedrock from Dún Laoghaire through County Wicklow, and into County Wexford, underlies the areas of Stillorgan and Ballinteer and it becomes clearly visible in features such as the Scalp, Rocky Valley, the Glen of the Downs and Glencree.

The granite from these mountains and valleys has been used by our earliest ancestors to build tombs for their dead: the early Christians built churches with it; medieval castles were built with it. These mountain valleys gave a place to retreat as well as a refuge for rebel families through centuries of attack.

Rathfarnham and Dundrum are located on the periphery of a fairly level plain of Carboniferous limestone, which is darkened by mud and shale. This limestone bedrock encircles and includes the city – extending from Merrion to Celbridge, on to the west to include the Phoenix Park and stretching to Swords on the north side.

Christian Corlett in his book *'Antiquities of old Rathdown'* explains some of the huge forces involved in shaping the landscape we see today.

"Towards the end of the Ice Age melted water formed enormous lakes, such as the one in the area of Fassaroe and Enniskerry. The sand and gravel deposited at the bottoms of these lakes formed a delta, and have been useful for quarrying in more recent times. The waters of this lake built up, being

trapped by the mountains to the west and the ice-sheets to the east in the Irish Sea. Eventually, the pressures created by the incredible volume of water found a weakness in the underlying bedrock and gouged out massive, steep valleys at the Rocky Valley, the Scalp and the Glen of the Downs. Today, their tiny streams are a slight testimony to the great flood-waters that created them."

Of course the rich mythology of Ireland paints a rather different, though equally dramatic, picture of the creation of Ireland and its people.

This mythology begins not only with a godly creation of land and people, but with the settling of Ireland. In his book *'Myth, Legend and Romance'*, Dr Daithi O hOgain, lecturer of Irish folklore at UCD describes the Fir Bolgs' arrival in an uninhabited Ireland. These were the descendants of a group of Nemedians who fled Greece for Ireland to escape the enslavement the Greeks had forced them to suffer. The Fir Bolg divided Ireland into five provinces, Connacht, Ulster, Leinster and the two Munsters. Folklore has it that they were the first invaders to establish administration of justice in Ireland.

The next invaders after the Fir Bolg were the Tuatha de Danaan, which means the people of the goddess Dana. They were supposed to have arrived amidst clouds and mist in the west of Ireland and in time were defeated in the Battle of Mag Tuiread. The Tuatha de Danaan were followed by the Milesians from Spain.

Whatever the level of truth contained within this folklore, archaelogical evidence points to the arrival of Middle Stone Age settlers who first settled immediately before 7000 BC, in the north-east of the country, which was rich in flint. Due to the work of archaeologists we know that south-east Dublin was first inhabited by hunters from the crude flint tools they left. These were known as 'Bann Flakes', which were first found in large numbers on the River Bann, but they were also found in Rathfarnham, Loughlinstown, and Dún Laoghaire. Other findings included remains of fish, birds and animal bones.

Some 3,000 years elapsed before the beginnings of agriculture with the clearing of woodlands, the creation of fields, and the division of the year into sowing and reaping divisions or seasons. These first farmers or Dolmen builders as they were occasionally known, built large tombs or dolmens for their dead. They were the first to leave their mark in this part of the country.

As part of the development for the Southern Cross route and the proposed housing development at Kingston, off Grange Road, Rathfarnham, excavations were carried out by Valerie Keeley in 1986-7. A number of artifacts dating to the Neolithic period were found in the townland of Kingston: a Megalithic tomb and holy well located in the vicinity of Taylors Grange and a further holy well at Ticknock.

This portal tomb, known as Brehon's Chair, consists of a burial chamber in which cremated human remains were placed, often with grave goods such as food vessels, and personal ornaments or stone implements. The chamber is characterized by one stone at the rear and two vertical stones at the front which form a type of portico with a doorstone blocking the entrance. This portal tomb was probably built c.3000 BC. The excavations also demonstrated that the chamber contained cremation burials, and the cairn contained a secondary burial accompanied by an inverted food vessel. It is interesting to note that eighteen of those twenty-seven megalithic tombs of County Dublin are located in the barony of Rathdown, mainly by the side of the mountains, beside streams and usually facing west.

Evidence of the people who superceeded these early Stone Age people in the Bronze Age period 4,500 years ago, has been provided by finds of beaker-pottery (the style of pottery used at that period). There is also evidence of wedge tombs of that period located on Two Rock Mountain, at Ballyedmonduff, Kilmashogue and Edmonstown near Rathfarnham which, according to archaeologists, indicate that the population was more widespread than during the Stone Age.

In due course these Bronze Age Irishmen were themselves displaced by incoming waves of Celtic Iron Age people from about 500 BC. It is not clear whether their arrival was deliberate invasion or a more gradual migration. In the next two centuries, the Bronze Age culture, their bronze weapons and tools being totally overmatched by those of the new arrivals, had disappeared. Although the Celts left a rich archeological heritage, the most obvious marks they left on the landscape were their ringforts. Evidence of these can be found at those place names with the prefix 'rath' like Rathfarnham, Rathgar and Rathmichael. Ringforts continued to be in use to almost the 17th century, being used as homes for farmers and their stock in latter centuries. There is widespread belief they are associated with the supernatural, in particular fairies. The townland of Killegar is known to have ten of these ringforts.

Although Celts and their culture were totally dominant throughout the country, they were not immune to radical cultural change themselves. This was particularly evident with the arrival of Christianity at the beginning of 5th century AD. This resulted in a flurry of church building which locally gave rise to the original St. Nahi's church which was established in the 7th century at Dundrum.

These early churches were fairly small rudimentary affairs built of wood or sometimes stone, but as the Christian Church assumed a central part of Celtic life, more elaborate arrangements came into being. The first monasteries were established and they soon gained great influence over the local communities in which they existed.

With that influence came wealth – a wealth which was to attract a people to these shores who would have a dramatic impact in the Dublin area.

The story of these people, the vikings, can be found in part two.

Dundrum

Dundrum was a rural village well outside the city bounds for much of the time since its establishment in the 15th century. Its commercial heart was located in the vicinity of the cross roads at the south-side of the village. It was to here at 'The Manor Mill' that local farmers brought their corn to be ground. Water was diverted from the local River Slang to form a large mill-pond. An overflow waterfall was also created to supply the industries in the valley below the castle. These were: three mill-wheels; a paper-mill run by Mrs Hall and an iron works run by a Mr Stokes.

In 1876, the Manor Mill was adapted to the Manor Mill Laundry, then the largest employer of female labour in the village. Work was collected from districts as far away as the town of Wicklow by both horse-drawn and motorised vehicles.

An advertisement which appeared in the Irish Times of 1917 stated… *"Manor Mill Laundry, County Dublin. Beautiful country situation, equaled only by the excellence of our work. Shirts and collars superbly finished. Washing by rail and post especially quoted for."* The charge for a detachable collar was 1d and for a shirt the charge was 4d. Each article had an indelible laundry-mark while the more important customers had their own wicker laundry baskets with code numbers, each packed with meticulous attention.

The laundry hooter sounded for a period of thirty seconds each morning at 7.50am, which was the 'get ready' signal and the final blast at 8am to commence work: again for lunch, a similar sound was heard at 1.50pm and 2pm. Street hawkers enlivened the residential roads as they carried on with their trade, calling, *"freestone"* (granite chips used for scouring), *"chairs to mend"* or *"umbrellas to mend"*.

This same village junction has, over the years, been the site for several well-known shops including Leverett & Fryes (agents for W. & A. Gilbey) who commenced business in 1896. Described as 'High Class' grocers and spirit merchants, they catered almost exclusively for the aristocracy of the village over several generations. This was a more leisurely age when the customer to L. & F. could linger a little longer over their weekly order with the undivided attention of the assistant. The week's gossip could be exchanged while you paid your bill – in cash – while you were still seated. However, this pleasant picture is not the full story, for shopping in the Dundrum of Victorian times had its own problems. The main shopping street was noisy and lively during the day with horse-drawn omnibuses, milk carts with large churns, delivery cars etc all trying to make their way through. On top of this, as in other villages of this period, the shopper had to contend with the dust from the street in the dry summer weather, and the mud and puddles when it rained – not easy for the women with their long skirts!

A key citizen of the time must have been the village post-master, William Mann who also attended to his second role as 'house & land agent' for twenty-five years until 1865, when his wife Jane took over as the post-mistress.

At the other end of the village through the last decade of the 1800s and early 1900s, James Collins was the proprietor of Uncle Tom's Cabin, then known as the *'Dundrum Tea-Gardens and Cyclist Rendezvous'*, perhaps reflecting the growing influence of the expanding city just down the road, an expansion which in the last few decades has imposed huge changes on Dundrum, as reflected in the following poem by a village resident in the early 1980s.

"O, Dundrum, how I love you, but you make me sad inside,
As I walk from Uncle Tom's Cabin on the road to Stepaside.
It's the rail bridge gone for ever,
It's the sound of the old steam train,
It's wave from the driver and fireman,
That has caused this terrible pain.

O Dundrum, how I love you, - you are getting very old,
Your graveyard on the Churchtown Road is now completely
closed.
The sloping hill where our dear ones sleep,
The River Slang running by their feet.
The rising sun - the wind - the sleet,
No more shall rouse them from their immortal sleep".

"The Castle of Dundrum, three miles south of Dublin, is inhabited and in excellent repair; at the north east end of it are the remains of a much older building than the present castle, which is visibly a modern addition in comparison to the old mansion. There is but very little of this ancient part remaining; some of the walls are six feet thick; about the castle are several traces of old walls, avenues etc. proving it to have once been a very complete habitation. The whole is on the summit of a small hill, surrounded by ash trees, with a handsome rivulet running at its foot but this shelter will soon be removed as they are cutting away trees".

This was how Austin Cooper, one of His Majesty's tax collectors, described the castle in the last decade of the 1700s.

Built by Richard Fitzwilliam in 1590, on the site of an earlier structure of the 13th century, the castle was one of the strategic defensive line of castles of Roebuck, Ballawley, Kilgobbin, Carrickmines and Kilternan enclosed within the Pale.

In 1619 the castle was awarded to another member of the family, William Fitzwilliam in recognition of his courageous defence against the assaults from the O'Byrnes and the O'Tooles who, since their expulsion from the area by Crown forces, had staged regular raids and attacks on the outskirts of the Pale from their bases in the mountains.

The Fitzwilliams, though representing the English Crown, were Catholic and the castle became one of the few refuges where a priest could stay in safety during the reigns of Elizabeth and James, and celebrate Mass for the local congregation of Dundrum.

Despite their support of the catholic cause the 300 year tenure of the Fitzwilliams was temporarilly interrupted when the castle was taken over by a local active group of insurgents in the Revolution of 1641, who then occupied it until January of the following year.

The transfer of the Fitzwilliam seat to Baggotrath and Merrion meant that Dundrum Castle was allowed to fall into disrepair after 1790, and with the passage of over two centuries only the shell of the castle remains, secluded from view due to recent extensions to the M50 motorway.

Dundrum Castle

"Only in popular education can man erect the structure of an enduring civilisation"… Andrew Carnegie.

Born in Scotland in 1835, Andrew Carnegie emigrated to the USA where his first job as a boy was in a cotton factory as a bobbin winder. By the time he was fifty he had his own steel works and was well on his way to becoming a millionaire.

During the last eighteen years of his life, Carnegie sponsored the building of 2,811 libraries, of which 660 were in Britain and Ireland. Besides Dundrum, the other areas in south County Dublin to benefit were: Dún Laoghaire, Shankhill, Cabinteely, Sandyford, Glencullen, Whitechurch and Stillorgan. The Dundrum building was opened in August 1914 by the then Lord Chancellor.

In the early years these Carnegie libraries were used as an entertainment centre for the community of the local village and Dundrum was no exception. The upper floor was equipped with a stage and a kitchen and it was a popular venue at which the local community gathered for their concerts,

dances, plays and sales-of-work. In the early 1920s, concerts were organised by Cathal McGarvey and the local organist, Mollie Gallagher, both of whom had Donegal roots. Irish step dancing classes were organised by 'Jem' Byrne and in the late 1920s the pantomime, *'Babes in the Wood'* was organised by the local dramatic group.

A preparatory school was conducted on the ground floor of the library during 1923-38 by Misses Carroll and Nesbit and Dundrum Vocational School classes had their beginnings at this library, prior to moving to a permanent location on the main street. The librarian through the 1940s and '50s was Miss May Courtney who served the community well into her advancing years.

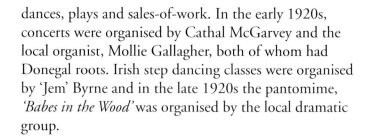

Carnegie Library

Established as far back as the 7th century the Church of St. Nahi has seen many alterations and work in its time, most notably in extensive restorations carried out in 1760 and again in 1910-14. This latter work is commemorated on a plaque which reads…

"The entrance gate to this Churchyard was erected by the parishioners of Taney Parish to the memory of William Monk Gibbon, Canon of Christ Church Cathedral by whose inspiration and effort the restoration of this church was accomplished. He repaired the altar of the Lord".

The font in St. Nahi's, transferred from St. Kevin's Parish Church, Dublin, was the one in which Arthur Wellesley, the Duke of Wellington was baptised in 1769. Many of the church furnishings include crafts by local well known artists – the central panel of the window which portrays the Annunciation was a work carried out by Evie Hone in 1926, and amongst other windows is the work of Harry Clarke who made a significant contribution to stained glass work in Ireland. The needlework picture over the altar is the work of Susan and Elizabeth Yeats (sisters of W.B. Yeats) and illustrates the Last Supper.

Two 17th century headstones described by Ball (an authorative local historian from Dundrum at the end of the 19th century) have disappeared from the adjacent cemetery, but twelve from the 18th century, and the remainder from the 19th and 20th centuries are still there. Details recorded in the *'Index to the Register of Burials'* for the parish during the twenty year period (January 1897 - April 1917) give a startling insight into life expectancy at that time. No less than 1,836 people were buried during this period and of these, 551 were children age six or under.

Until recently, St. Nahi's Church commanded an excellent view of the Dundrum village, but now the new suspension bridge under construction on the north-side entry to the village will tower over both.

St. Nahi's Church

According to Elrington Ball's book entitled, *'A History of the County Dublin'* (1903), Taney, as an ecclesiastical centre, dates back to the 13th century. It was then an extensive deanery with links to the parishes of Coolock, Chapelizod and Clonsilla. It also had chapels at Donnybrook, Rathfarnham and Kilgobbin.

The idea to replace the smaller old church with a larger parish church was first mooted in 1809. As the loan from the Board of First Fruits proved inadequate, other ideas of fund raising were discussed. One of these was the sale by auction of pew sites. The sale of eighteen pew sites on the ground, and eight on the gallery raised the sum of £384.10s. The seats were to be numbered in brass. William Farrell was the Diocesan architect for the church, which opened on Sunday 21 June 1818.

The Parliamentary Gazetteer of Ireland (1846) carried the following report on the Church of Christ Church, Taney…

"The modern Church is a spacious fabric, surmounting elevated ground, serving as a landmark to mariners and commanding very fine views over the city, the bay and a lovely expanse of country, the numerous ornamental plantations, of which combine, at this point of the observation, into a massive richness. The edifice itself, however, is as artistically defective as it is pretending and substantial".

The same observation might be similar to-day. The square bell-tower in the centre of the north-side of the church has created a prominent feature for the parish of Taney, the village of Dundrum, and surrounding areas, especially during the festive season of Christmas with its illuminated tree erected on the turret.

Christ Church, Taney

The Pembroke Estate was more concerned in their house design with quality rather than economy. Low rates were not a major priority. According to Mary Daly… *"The cottages erected by Pembroke Urban District Council were amongst the best provided by any Irish local authority. Rathmines again economised…."*.

Government Acts (1828 and 1854) provided Dublin suburbs with a framework for local home rule. Each suburb would be free to order its own affairs as it saw fit with little interference from Dublin Castle. This was the foundation for the establishment of townships. Rathmines, the first to take advantage of this legislation, was followed by other suburbs. The driving force behind these local authorities was generally the local landowners or local developers.

The land surrounding Dublin City was owned by a variety of landowners, the largest tract of land belonging to the Pembroke Estate, which extended from Merrion Square to Blackrock, Mount Merrion and Dundrum. The Pembroke township was established in 1863, followed by the setting-up of the Pembroke Urban District Council.

This council soon set about the erection of houses for the estate workers at Donnybrook, Merrion, Ringsend, Booterstown and in the village of Dundrum. House plans were drawn up and a local builder (most likely one John Richardson) was chosen. His monogram *W.R. 1881* can be found mounted on a plaque, located on the Kilmacud Road side of the building, once occupied by the Hazletts.

Twenty-six in all were built with granite from Barnacullia, and stock bricks from the brickworks. In the early 1900s, the weekly rent of 2s 9d was paid to the Pembroke Estate: a rent that was considered expensive in comparison with similar cottages in adjoining villages. The six built beside the Pye Complex were purchased for £600 by the Manor Mill Laundry for its workers.

Pembroke Cottages

Airfield, an 18th century farmhouse, was purchased in 1894 by a Dublin solicitor, Trevor Overend, who carried out improvements to the house with the addition of a library with a Jacobean-style ceiling.

Trevor Overend and his wife had two daughters, Letitia and Naomi. The period in which the Overend girls grew up was marked by the coming of women's emancipation in 1918 – the year on which Naomi completed her education at Alexandra College, Milltown. While neither of the girls were actively involved in the Suffragette movement, the life-long interests of these two sisters in mechanics, motoring and farming suggest emancipation of a sort!

Trevor Overend died in 1919, the year Letitia bought her first Ford car, which was soon followed by other models. Mrs Overend bought herself a two-seater Peugeot Quadrilette at Dawson Street, Dublin for £200.

In 1927 Mrs Overend and her two daughters went to London where Letitia was looking for a tourer car. She paid £1,750 for a 1926 Rolls Royce which was a returned 'unwanted gift'. So enamoured were the girls with this car that they served their time at Rolls Royce to enable them to do all the maintenance on the car themselves, not trusting their pride and joy to anyone else.

It was a frequent sight in Dundrum to see Letitia park her Rolls in the middle of the street outside the grocery shop, attract the shop-assistant with a blast of the car-horn and then sit and wait for her shopping while the local Gárda Síochana on duty would turn a blind eye!

In parallel with their mechanical prowess the Overend sisters were also widely known for their organic farming/gardening skills and kept a prize herd of Jersey cows.

The Misses Overend lived until the early 1990s. Because there was no family to inherit Airfield the Overends formed a trust to manage the future of the estate for the people of Dublin.

Today the Airfield staff include a botanist and archivist and the Airfield Trust is open daily to the connoisseur of home-cooked food, the traditional farm and garden enthusiast, and those interested in vintage cars.

In the first decade of the 19th century notices for accommodation appeared in the National Press. The Freeman's Journal of February 27th 1813 carried the following notice…

"Meadowbrook Boarding House Dundrum….the second whey season having commenced, Ladies and Gentlemen are respectfully informed that there are a few vacancies in the house: accommodation will be found agreeable, and the terms very much reduced - respectable society in the house".

Such adverts reflected Dundrum's role at the time as a healthy retreat for those wishing to escape the overcrowded confines of Dublin. The village and its surrounding area was valued for its fresh air as well as several other healthy commodities, in particular fresh goat's milk products from the many goats grazing the surrounding hills at that time.

To cater for these escapees from the city a regular coach service between Dublin and Dundrum commenced in 1816. The service was organised by Robert Turbett, who drew up the following plan, from which he made a profit of £300 annually...

"PROSPECTUS of a plan for running coaches between Dublin, Dundrum, and Enniskerry, with a calculation of Expenses and Income etc.".

"One coach to leave Dublin every morning for Enniskerry and return to Dublin from Enniskerry every evening….It is supposed that the coach to Enniskerry would be filled by persons going to see the County of Wicklow, the Dargle Waterfall, etc. and returning from them, and by persons going in the morning to Dundrum to drink Goat's Whey. The Dundrum Coach to Dublin in the morning would be filled by persons living in Dundrum going to Dublin on business, and by those who came out in the Enniskerry Coach to drink Goat's Whey".

In time the coach service was supplemented with the establishment of a railway, linking the village with Dublin. This was known as 'The Dundrum and Rathfarnham Railway' which afterwards merged into the Dublin Wicklow scheme. The line from Harcourt Street to Bray was finally opened on July 10th, 1854. The Dublin Evening Post of July 11th reported on an inspection carried out on the line as… *"A rich treat was on Saturday afforded to the shareholders of the Dublin and Wicklow Railway, and their friends…each train conveyed 200 persons".*

Meadowbrook House

Originally known as Primrose Hill, this grand house was built in the latter part of the 18th century with Hon. John Butler, MP for Newcastle, as its first occupier, until he died in 1790. By the time Samuel Lewis, the famous travel writer, described it in the early 19th century as *"a handsome residence containing a richly stored museum of natural curiosities"*, its name had changed to 'Wyckham'.

The residents of this property, over the following fifty years, were mainly families of the legal profession like John White, William Farran and Leonard Bickerstaff. Sir Robert Kane MD, and his family were the occupants for the period of 1856-73. Despite his long commitment to the setting up of Queen's College, Cork (UCC) which entailed frequent trips to Cork, Sir Robert conceded to the love of his wife Catherine (nee Bailey) by remaining at Wyckham which she loved so dearly.

The Simpson's Hospital, by which the building is known today, originates with one George Simpson. As a young man he left his home in Kildare to walk to Dublin to seek his fortune. He spent his first night sleeping on the doorstep of a drapery shop in Henry Street. The following morning George was found by the shop owner who took him in, fed him, listened to his story and gave him a job which he held for a number of years. In the best storybook fashion George in time became a well-known merchant in the city.

George and his wife Catherine resided at Stoneybatter, Prussia Street, and finally at Jervis Street. According to his will, he donated the bulk of his fortune to the establishment of a hospital … *"and thereto to erect and support and maintain a hospital for such poor decayed, blind and gouty men as they shall think worthy of such a charity"*. Simpson's Hospital was established in 1779 adjacent to where William's & Woods was located at Parnell Street. In 1925, this hospital was transferred to Wyckham, where it continued to provide care for forty-five male residents after almost two and a quarter centuries.

Simpson's Hospital

The design for this elaborate Victorian residence was drawn up in 1860 by the architect John Skipton Mulvaney. It was for a particular client and because of the number of projects he had in progress, it took the architect ten years to complete this ornate dwelling. It included a tower house which has been described as an extremely well-built stone structure of authentic medieval appearance. The first residents at Gortmore were Richard Atkinson and his wife. Richard predeceased his wife by three years and he was buried at St. Nahi's graveyard.

As soon as Edward Burke, a wealthy wine and foreign spirit export merchant, took up residence in 1884, he spared no time with his extensive plans for alterations. Traces of Burke's initials (E.B.) are to be seen on the newel posts of the impressive oak staircase in the stately interior of Gortmore.

Other additions and modifications which were introduced during the residency of Burke included billiard and smoking rooms. The idea of introducing the garden into the house was a feature of the 19th century, and this was carried out by Burke in the form of the erection of an impressive domed conservatory.

Burke's residence was followed by John Gardiner Nutting, a relative and chairman of the Burke business. Other occupants included such family names as Macready, Sir Joseph Redmond, Hegarty, Dudgeon and LeFroy.

Gortmore, with its fifty acres of land was finally sold for £12,000 by Mr B. St George LeFroy to the Order of Carmelites in March 1944. The name was soon altered from Gortmore to Gort Muire. Its initial function was as a Novitiate, later as a House of Studies in the early 1960s and more recently as a Conference Centre.

GORTMORE

Rathfarnham

The placename 'Rathfarnham' is believed to date from about 50 BC. Many interpretations have been given to its meaning including *'a dweller in the ferns'*. But P.W. Joyce's suggestion that the meaning is derived from *'Rath Fearnain'*, or *'Rath of the Alders'* would seem to be the most appropriate: as alder trees still grow on the banks of the Dodder – the river overlooking where the Rath once stood.

The writer Ball has the following to say in the context of the village…
"The village of Rathfarnham at the end of the 18th century was said by Austin Cooper to be a small village with very few houses of the better class, and the residents in the neighbourhood were not numerous". The most accurate population figure for the village was 644 in 1841. This figure increased to 1,065 within twenty years, and then gradually tapered off to 415 by 1911.

Lewis described the village scene of 1837 as follows…

"At the commencement of the Insurrection of 1798, the village was the scene of a skirmish between a detachment of the King's troops and a party of insurgents, in which several of the latter were killed and others taken prisoner. Near the village is a lofty bridge of a single arch over the river Dodder, the road from which is thickly shaded by the plantations of the demesnes on each side: the place itself is a long straggling street with very little to attract attention…Petty Sessions are held in the village every Wednesday. It has a

metropolitan police station and has a dispensary: a fair is held in it on the 10th of July".

The family name of Taylor is associated with Rathfarnham village and surrounding areas, especially Alderman Thomas Taylor. He lived in the vicinity since the late 1690s and his family name has been associated with such place names as Taylor's Grange, Taylor's Lane and Taylor's Hill. Robert, a descendant, described himself as…

"I'm the knockabout of Rathfarnham,
but you know who I am…
I am the Yella Bob,
And I sit in the Yella trap,
And I drive the Yella pony,
To the Yella House,
To spend the Yella money
On the Yella Whiskey".

The village was well endowed with every natural advantage with its high elevation, affording a magnificent view of the Dublin mountains as well as an abundance of fresh air. As the 18th century arrived, advantage was taken of these convalescent features. The village hosted numerous visitors from the city for the healthy and therapeutic properties of the locality, which became a favourite resort for the high society of the day. A spa was discovered and the visitors arrived in great numbers to drink these waters.

An omnibus, drawn by two horses, served the village from Dublin in the 1840s. These vehicles carried twelve passengers on the inside, and ten on the outside. An 'inside' fare to Rathfarnham cost six pence while the cost of an 'outside' fare was four pence. During the 1860s, an attempt to provide a rail link was unsuccessful.

There was also a pedestrian link between the villages of Dundrum and Rathfarnham. This route took the traveller around the perimeter of estates, through Nolan's Avenue, via *'The Dairies'*, and through the *'Narrow Lanes'*. These passageways, with their six-metre high walls on either side, passed opposite 'The Yellow House' towards the village. These Avenues and Lanes, which divided the estates and linked villages are no longer in existence.

At the approach to the village, the old Protestant cemetery can be seen: in it stands the remaining gable of a ruined church which predates the church close by, which was built in 1783. It is believed that a church stood on this site from Norman times.

Built initially as a fortified mansion for Archbishop Loftus, Lord Chancellor of Ireland in 1585, it was used as a garrison outpost to defend the City of Dublin against the regular raids by the O'Byrnes and the O'Tooles from the Wicklow mountains and in the 1641 uprising it served as a strongpoint for the forces of the Crown.

At the time when properties were taxed according to the number of heating fires in the building, the castle was rated as containing eighteen hearths. Amongst those who were in occupancy in the early 1700s were the following: George Hopkins, William Denison, George Gasborough, William Dixon, Anthony Poulter, David Gibson, Daniel Reading, Laurence Hudson and others.

Writing in 1837, Lewis describes the layout of this castle as follows…

"The castle, now the property of the Marquess of Ely, is a large and stately mansion in the centre of a fine and thickly planted demesne, the principal entrance to which is a very beautiful gateway, built in the style of a Roman triumphal arch, besides which there is a very lofty pointed Gothic gateway leading to the village: entrance to the house from the terrace on which it stands is by a portico of eight Doric columns which support the dome painted in fresco with signs of the zodiac: the great hall is ornamented…".

Little is known of the castle during the first half of the 19th century. A fire insurance mark is still to be seen fixed to the external walls, indicating that a policy was in force in 1807. Lord Chancellor Blackburne was in occupation during the years 1847-52 when 'modern conveniences' like bathrooms were installed with other modifications. In 1913, the castle was purchased the Jesuit Order, which sold it to the Office of Public Works, later being declared a National Monument.

Rathfarnham Castle

Local folklore has it that the original tavern bearing the name *'Yellow House'* dates to the mid 18th century when it was then located, as a thatched house, standing on the site occupied by the present Catholic Church.

In the records of the 1798 Rebellion by the United Irishmen, Rathfarnham is mentioned as having a number of minor uprisings during which time two of its residents were hanged at Queen's Bridge on May 26th 1798. One of those, Ledwich, was a brother of the P.P. of Rathfarnham, the other was a man called Wade. They were buried at Croppy's Acre.

In the years following the rebellion Michael Eades and his family, the proprietors of the Yellow House were suspected of Republican sympathies and treasonable practices. The frequent visits of wanted United Irishmen fugitives to the Yellow House at the time would seem to confirm these suspicions. Among these were Michael Dwyer and Arthur Devlin who were on the run and were later jailed for their activities in 1798. They would sit in the Yellow House where they could eavesdrop on the soldiers from Castle as they plotted to capture the pair of them.

Eventually Michael Eades was convicted of being part of the United Irishmen movement and in 1803, by way of retribution the Yellow House was wrecked. However, within twenty years of being razed to the ground the village tavern was rebuilt by a Mary Murphy on the current site in 1825. It opened for business in 1827 and played a big part in the social life of the Rathfarnham residents, serving as a centre for Irish dancing competitions and story telling, as well as a hostillery for those who attended the fairs.

The Yellow House was purchased in 1912 by the Walker family. Initially, the premises were used for the sale of groceries and hardware, though it was also a preferred place to socialise over a drink. Patrick Walker enlarged these popular premises during the sixty-five years of the Walker occupancy. The Durkin brothers next bought the premises, which later became part of a consortium.

The Yellow House

Over two hundred years ago Joseph Archer, the well-known Dublin historian, described Marlay and its house as follows...

"The house is extremely elegant, the gardens are handsome and extensive, and contain a good deal of glass, the whole abounding with a variety of fruit. The demesne is beautifully laid out with fine walks, well wooded, remarkably well watered and skillfully planted, and the whole well enclosed with a good stone wall"

The description given at the time of its auction in 1853 was that of an...

"Excellent well arranged residence, sufficiently large for the accommodation of a family, without being an encumbrance...And from its proximity to Dublin, and being surrounded by the aristocratic neighbourhoods of Dundrum, Rathmines and Rathfarnham renders it one of the most desirable for... villa residences, leaving a sufficient quantity of land with the mansion and without at all interfering with its privacy".

In the meantime, Marlay has changed. The Dún

Laoghaire–Rathdown County Council acquired the three hundred acre demesne and house in 1972 for £1M. The development of Marlay was a challenge for the designers to bring it to what it is today. The demesne and house has been used to shoot scenes for films such as *'Strumpet City'* and *'Benedict Arnold'*.

Previous residents at Marlay included the families of Thomas Taylor in the late 17th century, Robert Tedcastle, the Dublin coal merchant and, in the early 1900s, Philip Love. The La Touche family line resided here during 1784-1884, and it was David La Touche who named the place Marlay after his wife Elizabeth, daughter of Rt. Rev. George Marlay, Bishop of Dromore.

"Early morning run through fresh woodlands, birds greeting, squirrels darting, graceful swans on lake, peace, tranquillity, sense of space and freedom, listening, breathing the beauty of Marlay Park".

Reflections by Tom Kitt, TD, former Minister for Labour and local resident.

Marlay

Patrick Pearse, an educational visionary at the turn of the century, founded his first school in Cullinswood House, at Ranelagh in September 1908. Two years later, the Hermitage (previously known as the Fields of Odin, Rathfarnham) came on the market with its thirty acres of woods and parks, rivers and a lake. It was purchased for £6,000, and St. Enda's, a school for seventy boys, opened in September 1910.

Inspiration for Pearse's type of school was Cuchulainn, the youthful warrior-hero of the sagas, who seemed to be the ideal embodiment of the virtues Pearse wanted to instill in his pupils. Amongst the mottos attributed to Cuchulainn, prominently displayed in the school were; *"Better is short life with honour than long life with dishonour"*, and *"I care not though I were to live one day and one night if only my fame and my deeds live after me"*. The children received a fully rounded educational experience in so far as each of their faculties received full consideration and attention.

Further insight into Pearse's philosophy in the education of children for life can be found in these words which were written for his school magazine (entitled *An Macaomh*) in 1909:

"One's life in a school is a perpetual adventure, and adventure among souls and minds; each child is a mystery, and if the plucking out of the heart of so many mysteries is fraught with much in labour and anxiety,

there are compensations richer than have ever rewarded any voyagers among treasure-islands in tropic seas."

The atmosphere of the grounds of St. Enda's was the essence of Pearse's approach to pupil learning, and his love and enthusiasm for the place can be clearly seen when he described his feelings in his poem, *'The Wayfarer'*

Sometimes my heart hath shaken with joy
To see a leaping squirrel in a tree,
Or a red lady-bird upon a stalk,
Or little rabbits in a field at evening
Lit by slanting sun,
Or some green hill where shadows drifted by…

St. Enda's

In the 13th century, the parish of Whitechurch was in the possession of St. Mary's Abbey before it later became part of the Tallaght parish. It was not until 1823 that Whitechurch was made a separate parish by Dr. Magee, Archbishop of Dublin. The ruins of the original church are located opposite the present parish church, which celebrates its 175th anniversary having been consecrated in June 1827.

The three streams which run through the parish of Whitechurch were once harnessed to run a number of mills in the neighbourhood. One mill owner, Andrew Moller, in the early 1760s donated a parcel of land for the Moravian cemetery, which is located close to the church. The first person to be buried there was John Tellschig, a native of Moravia from where the Moravian doctrine originated in 1457.

"In essentials, unity; in nonessentials, liberty; and in all things, love", is the motto of the Moravian belief. Formerly known as Unitas Fratrum: they pondered on the principles of The Sermon on the Mount to form a basis for their beliefs. The religion soon spread to London, and in 1746 John Cennick, the Moravian Evangelist visited Dublin at the invitation of Benjamin Latrobe, a Moravian preacher and graduate of Trinity College.

The Dublin Moravian congregation ceased to exist in December 1980 due to a decision of the Synod of the British Province in July 1980. The Irish District of the Moravian Church consists in five centres which are located mainly in Counties Antrim and Down.

In the cemetery itself the main two-metre wide footpath divides the 120 metre long burial ground into two parts. Males are buried on the right side and females on the left side. This serene and relaxed resting place, surrounded by shrubs and trees, contains 650 memorials each lying flat, level with the ground.

Whitechurch Parish Church

In 1720, William Connolly, speaker at the House of Commons, purchased some lands from the Loftus estate on the summit of Mount Pellier Hill. He set about building a house utilising stones as materials from an adjacent large cairn. His intention was that it would contain a number of rooms including servants' quarters and that he would use this as a hunting-lodge. This was an elegant residence with a grand flight of stone steps leading to the hall door.

Shortly after completion, the slated roof was blown off one night during a violent storm. This was seen by local residents as divine retribution, as they believed that the builder had behaved in a sacrilegious manner by desecrating the cairn. However, Connolly was determined that this setback should not affect his intentions and so reinforced the building with an arched roof on the principle of a bridge. Despite this robust construction his tenure did not last long and within a couple of years, Connolly vacated the house, which fell into decay. The stone steps were removed and used for Lord Ely's lodge, which was the entrance to Rathfarnham Castle.

During the 1730s the Hellfire Club movement, already banned by the Government in England for its extreme views on religion, had set up a branch in Dublin. The club members held regular meetings at the Eagle Tavern, near Dublin Castle. Perhaps seeking a more secluded base, the members of the Club set about the restoration of what remained of the lodge on Mount Pellier Hill.

This location then became a base for their meetings and it soon became known as 'The Hellfire Club'. Many rumours spread in the vicinity about what went on there, like the celebration of Black Masses as well as the keeping of a black cat on the premises as Satan's representative.

Legend has it that, in a scene worthy of a Hollywood horror film, a young clergyman crossing the Dublin mountains one night sought refuge at the house during a snowstorm, believing the building to be no more than a farmhouse. It was only after the door was opened by a cloaked figure brandishing a sword, did he realize his dreadful mistake. On entering he found the club members having a meal, the guest of honour being a black cat. On discovering the significance of the cat, the clergyman attempted to exorcise it. But the cat jumped onto the overhead chandelier, which fell, setting the house alight and burning it to the ground.

Meetings ceased to be held and the club was disbanded in 1741 following the death of one of its members, Richard Parsons, the first Earl of Rosse.

The Hellfire Club

Kilakee House, overlooking the city of Dublin, was built in the 18th century as a dower house for the Massey family. It is situated on the side of Kilakee Mountain (390 metres high) once known as *'White Sands Mountain'* due to the quantity of quartz found there. The combined action of rain and wind over the years has carved the mountain peat into unusual shapes, and in the course of the ages, the granite surface has disintegrated leaving just grains of quartz, with occasional garnets which are too small to be of any value. On the summit of the hill, behind Kilakee House, is the fire-ravaged ruins of what remains of the Dublin Hellfire Club.

The story of this house has a disturbed past with a number of stories of hauntings which this house experienced, readily retold by locals. One of those was concerned with the nightly appearance of a black cat, lurking in the undergrowth of the garden. The animal was described as 'the size of a biggish dog with terrible eyes'. According to the tales, this cat-like monster seemed to have lived for some forty years and was later portrayed in a well known oil painting 'Black Cat of Kilakee' by Tom McAssey, a local Dunlin artist, who apparently had seen this beast.

Kilakee House lay derelict for a number of years after World War II, but was purchased by Mrs Margaret O'Brien in the late 1960s for the purpose of exhibiting of works of art by Irish artists and sculptors.

It would seem that a combination of interacting factors including the resurgance of interest in the mystic during the late 1960s may have led to the resurrection of the old stories. Whatever the reason, Kilakee House became the centre of what was apparently a veritable storm of psychic activity in the late 1960s and early 1970s. The onset of the phenomena occurred when new residents moved into the house and ended when they left.

Kilakee Country House Restaurant

The locality of Cruagh was described by Lewis as follows….

'This parish is situated on the river Owendugher, a branch of the Dugher or Dodder river, by which it is separated from the parish of Whitechurch; and comprises 4,762 statute acres, of which 2,400 are mountain, including 400 acres of good acres. Killakee, the residence of S. White Esq., is a spacious mansion, situated in a tastefully embellished demesne, with a well-wooded glen through which a mountainous stream rushes with great force over its rocky bed; and surrounded by a winding road, several miles in circuit commanding some magnificent views of the City and bay of Dublin, with the hill of Howth, Ireland's Eye, of the mountain of Mourne in the distance which are distinctly visible in clear weather…'

The watch tower, a grim reminder of the past, stands partly on the site of the church on a steep slope surrounded by a high wall, which encloses the old cemetery of over ninety headstones. There is a chamber below ground-level with access to the upper chambers. The openings on the upper part of the outer wall gave a wide view of the surrounding countryside – vitally important given that the function of this tower was to protect the cemetery from body snatchers.

Prior to the Anatomy Act of 1832, there was a serious shortage of human bodies for dissection both here, and in the UK. The only solution to make up for this shortfall was to go out in the dark of night and dig up a hopefully fresh corpse. This was carried out by either medical students or by professional body snatchers who were known by various names like resurrectionists, 'sack-'em-up men' or stiffy lifters. The Dublin Gazette carried various reports of such incidents in the 1750s.

Cruagh
Watchtower

Olivia Hayes

This massive well-known granite landmark is situated equidistant between Barnacullia to the north, and Two Rock Mountain to the south. The 520 metres high feature commands a spectacular panoramic view of the surrounding counties from Lambay Island to Slieve Gullion in County Armagh. It has been described by such eminent people as Gabriel Beranger in 1780, and in 1835 by the painter and archaeologist G. V. Du Noyer. Writers of the past tended to regard mountains as objects of horror, being inhabited by monsters and evil spirits. Mountains were not looked to as places to visit – almost the opposite of today when the Three Rock Mountain has a strong appeal for those many hill walkers who derive pleasure in the wilds of the hills of south County Dublin.

However, Lewis' description seems to capture its association with the history of that part of the barony of Rathdown, and it reads as…

"This rugged and almost inaccessible tract of country seemed for five centuries a barrier of nature, that English laws or armies could not penetrate, and while the O'Byrnes, with a vigilance that never slept, maintained the fastness of their own territory unaffected by the encroachment of the Palesmen. This, the intervening district was resigned by both parties to as a theatre of hostility, which neither side would cultivate nor even inhabit".

This mountainous part of south County Dublin was frequently referred to as *'O'Byrnes Country'*. The last chief of this clan, Fiach Mac Hugh O'Byrne, was killed in a skirmish in 1597. This clan attempted to live up to its motto - certavi et vici - which is *"I have fought and conquered"*. Linked to this family, and its frequent raiding activities, were their 'cousins', the O'Toole Clan. These frequent incursions and raids extended over a period of three hundred years from the 17th century.

Three Rock Mountain

The 18th century village of Glencullen is situated high on the southern slopes of Two Rock Mountain, and its aspect can often be very exposed and sometimes bleak. Lying within the Dublin mountains, Glencullen is the meeting point of the Counties Dublin and Wicklow.

The focal point at this village cross-roads is Johnny Fox's pub, which is almost unchanged since the time of Daniel O'Connell, the great Irish Liberator, who lived at Glencullen, and used to be a regular visitor. O'Connell favoured this venue as one of his safe 'meeting places'.

The travel writer Curry tells of a interesting well which was situated a quarter of a mile west of Glencullen House near the river. He says that the peasantry call it the "Butter Well" as they believed that washing dairy vessels with its water is a particular invocation against the loss of butter by witchcraft. The well was located on Fiery Lane, which is said to be the early site of Glencullen village.

Glencullen became a Catholic stronghold in the 19th Century for the native Irish families. The O'Tooles and the O'Byrnes had been driven from Dublin into the mountains some centuries earlier. It was from here they continued to raid the well-cultivated lands of south County Dublin from Norman times.

"There are no strangers here, only friends who have not yet met", is an example of one of the many inscriptions to be seen on the walls of this well-known establishment, which is one of Dublin's oldest pubs. It was established in 1798 and is reckoned to be 'The Highest Pub above Sea level'.

Today's clientele is a rare mixture of chatty locals side by side with tourists of all types including visiting Presidents, Royalty, Ambassadors, Actors and Sports Personalities, as well as the energetic people absorbed in the pleasure of walks through the Dublin and Wicklow mountains.

Johnny Fox's Pub

Lewis gives a rather poetic description of the countryside scenery on the road to Enniskerry, with particular reference to what he refers to as *"the remarkable pass called the Scalp"*. His description is as follows…

"The mountains at Glencullen abound with grouse. On the road to Enniskerry, and within two miles of that beautiful village, is the Scalp, a deep natural chasm in the mountain, forming a narrow defile with lofty and shelving ramparts on each side, from which large detached masses of granite of many tons weight have fallen".

This picturesque natural feature was formed on the west by the rocky heights of Killegar and on the east by the wooded hill of Barnaslingan. The surprising fact about this impressive ravine of The Scalp is the absence of a stream running through it. The reason is that The Scalp was formed at the end of the Ice Age. Ice sheets covering these hills melted back northwards releasing vast amounts of water. The ice sheets were thick, and temporarily prevented drainage northwards. Trapped meltwater eroded a channel through the ridge of hills as it flowed in a southward direction.

Hillwalking enthusiasts follow a path from the northside approach to The Scalp, through furze and heather, to reach a grassy vantage point. A panoramic picture of the surrounding countryside may be experienced from this peak of 275 metres high: the scene would include the Two and Three Rock Mountains, Glencullen Valley, Bray Head as well as the Great and Little Sugar Loafs.

And for the passing visitor, on the road to Enniskerry, Lewis gives a further more detailed description of The Scalp….

"On each side, large masses of detached rock are heaped together in the wildest confusion, apparently arrested in their descent, and threatening every moment to crush the traveller by their fall".

The Scalp

Olivia Hayes

Built by the Walsh family, the location of this early Norman castle was strategically positioned on the edge of the Pale. Its main function was to defend the city from the frequent raids of the Wicklow families. The castle was a centre of military activity, and as such was larger than most tower houses, as forces of varying sizes were stationed there through the early years. Members of the Walsh family lines married into other landlord families in south County Dublin like the Eustaces, the Fitzwilliams and the Barnwells. In the early 1600s Theobald Walsh kept a priest and a friar to celebrate Mass.

The Walsh family and their Carrickmines Castle were eloquently described by Ball as follows...

"At the beginning of the seventeenth century, the Walshes were described as a large and ancient stock, and as men of note in the metropolitan county, which was then rich and plenteous in corn and cattle, and inhabited by a people of stately port and garb. The castle of Carrickmines was surrounded by an orchard and a garden, and, so far as was possible, its lands had been subjected to the plough".

During the Rebellion of 1641 the Walshes changed sides, and led a revolt against the English. In March 1642 the Government force, led by Sir Simon Harcourt, laid siege on the castle. There are varying accounts of this, but it seems that at least three hundred of the occupants were killed. The castle was blown up and then leveled to the ground.

A fragment of this castle remained, and later formed the end wall of a piggery for the Mooney family who lived there until August 2001 when excavation of the site commenced. This extensive excavation has been in preparation for the completion of the remaining part of the South Eastern section of the M50 motorway.

Carrickmines Castle

At the entrance to the old cemetery is a three metre high granite cross which was found buried in the cemetery in the middle of the last century. It has been described as a Maltese formed cross, with its left arm broken off and lost. Frequently referred to as "The Kilgobbin Cross", it has been estimated as dating from the 10th century because the length of the garment covering the figure of Christ is ankle length.

The remains of an 18th century church occupy a scenic position on this elevated site. It was in use until 1826 and is now maintained by the Office of Public Works. The ruins of this church overlook both the new cemetery at Kilgobbin as well as the adjoining old cemetery where Edmund Darley of nearby Fern Hill as well as Richard (Boss) Croker of Glencairn are buried.

Croker had a colorful history both while alive as well as after death. His wife refused to grant her husband a divorce, emigrated to the U.S. and died there in September 1914. Boss attended her funeral and returned to Ireland in a few weeks with his new bride, Beulah Edmonson, a Cherokee Indian princess. On his death in 1922, Richard's wish that his remains be interred beside those of his horse Orby (which had won the Epsom Derby) was not observed and he was interned in his private chapel at Glencairn in an unusual casket which had a window on one side.

On his death, 'Boss' Croker bequeathed Glencairn to his wife Beulah for life and to the Sisters of Charity. This arrangement didn't work out as a prolonged litigation caused bankruptcy. Bills had to be paid etc. and Glencairn was finally sold to the O'Neill family who, unhappy to have the shades of the previous owner around, had the remains of 'Boss' removed, and reinterred at Kilgobbin cemetery with his former housekeeper, Stella Bowman – perhaps appropriate if the rumours of the time about their relationship were to be believed.

Also in Kilgobbin graveyard is the unmarked grave which contains the remains of Honour Bright (known as Lizzie O'Neill) whose unclaimed body was found lying on the road at nearby Ticknock on 9th June 1925. The tragic tale of her life and the suspicious circumstances surrounding her death were the talk of the entire country at the time.

Kilgobbin Cemetery

These early Cistercian monks had no tenants or serfs: they relied on the labour of their own hands to work the land. Their austere lives, their poverty, and love of solitude had a particular appeal in an Irish context because they reminded people of the severe lives of the early Irish saints. As the monks had the obligation to chant the complete Divine Office daily, they could never work far away from the Abbey. Lay brothers had been introduced so the monks would be free to dwell within the cloister, and attend to the duties of the choir.

Kilternan Abbey, and its surrounding land were originally held by the monks of St. Mary's Abbey as a country residence and a farm. These white monks erected a manor house, which they occupied from time to time and it was most likely in connection with their residence there that, at the close of the 13th century, an accusation was brought against the Abbot of the Abbey. According to Francis E. Ball, a County Dublin historian in the early 20th century, it seems that the Abbot was using various mechanical devices such as snares and nets as well as greyhounds to catch wild beasts in the Crown forests of Glencree. The Crown authorities took action against him but later dropped the case. One can only speculate what the tabloids would make of it today!

Wakeman, in the Royal Society of Antiquaries of Ireland describes the abbey as follows… *This Cill or Teampull is the form of a plain oblong quadrangle, measuring externally 54 feet by 24 feet. It retains three features viz. an original square-headed doorway in the southside wall, and a round-headed light to the east. It is evident that the whole of the fabric, with the exception of the eastern gable and portion of the adjoining side walls, is of very early date".* The doorway on the southern side wall is 13th century origin, and designed to replace the original square headed one in the west gable. There is a round, hollowed and perforated stone, supposed to have been a baptismal font, lying within the ruin and the holy well of St. Tiernan stands close at hand.

Kilternan Abbey

Olivia Hayes

The first mention of Fernhill occurred in the Ordnance Survey Name Books of 1836 where it is referred to as Fearn Hill. Speculation was that of an Anglicization of Fearain Coille, 'wooded townland'.

At the end of the 18th and beginning of the 19th century, the major landowner in the area was Sir William Verner of Verner's Bridge, County Armagh. The Verners had acquired land in various parts of Ireland and England through commerce, inheritance and settlement for military service to the Crown, and by 1850 they owned 2,000 acres (including Fernhill) of the townlands surrounding Rathdown.

William Frederick Darley was the first member of the Darley family to be in possession of Fernhill. It was purchased from Sir Edmund Verner in 1893-94 under the Land Purchase Acts. Edmund Saunders Darley, the last member of the family, died in 1912 and his wife Mabel Elizabeth inherited the demesne although spent the latter part of her life with her daughter in England. In 1934, Fernhill was purchased by Joseph Walker for the sum of £3,500.

The Walker family descended from a long line of farmers and landowners of Ballygar, County Roscommon. The estate continues to the present day, down through the Walker family line to the present Sally Walker who was awarded by An Taisce with a special Environment recognition, and again in 1994 the RHSI presented a Silver Medal of Honour in recognition of the Walkers' contribution to horticulture in Ireland. Fernhill has been acknowledged by the Office of Public Works as a Heritage Garden.

Fernhill

Olivia Hayes

For over two centuries this Sanyford Inn as it was known, was on the main Chatham Street to Enniskerry Mail Coach journey. It was a period that echoed the nostalgic sounds of harness-bells and hoof-beats as stage coaches came and went. The Inn was one of its stopping points for travellers to quench their thirst.

For a century, it was also the village post office where the mail was deposited for the Sandyford region. The MacFarlane's, mill owners with English connections, were the original landlords for 130 years. Rose Skehan, manager of the local Leopardstown mart, bought Sandyford House in 1895 for £500, and appointed her sister Catherine Lindsay with her husband Albert as caretakers of the premises. Four years later, Rose died intestate: the Lindsays carried on with the business for a further ten years until they sold it to D. P. Flavin for £690 from which £150 went to the Lindsays, and the remainder to pay off the debts.

Business was certainly boosted with the regular visits from Richard Croker, the flamboyant resident at nearby Glencairn. He was better known as 'Boss' and frequently arrived in his chauffeur driven Packard V12 car, which he had imported from the United States. The turnover on the premises soared for weeks in June 1907 due to his generosity to locals when his horse Orby was to first ever Irish horse to win the Epsom Derby.

After the death of D. P. Flavin in December 1937, Sandyford House was then referred to as *'Widow Flavin's'*. In 1949, the widow's daughter Joan married Michael Walsh: the Walsh family line has continued to the present owner Myles Walsh, who was previously a successful showjumper.

Sandyford House

Stillorgan Village

A description of Stillorgan village was given by Dalton in 1836 as follows…

"Stillorgan maybe characterised as a village of better order, consisting of a street of houses, principally slated. Here was formerly the residence of Lord Carrysfort to whose heir the fee belongs. At the entrance into the church yard are poor schools, one for boys at which forty-five are educated, and one for girls at which thirty-five are educated. There is likewise an infant's school. They are all supported by private contributions. Mr Darley has a brewery in the village. It stood at the corner of Brewery Road. A dispensary was established in 1828".

150 years later, a village resident had the following observations to make…

*'The village has seen some changes in its time;
The roar of rushing cars is never still
past the long row of cottages that
climb, Backed by tall trees, the
steep Stillorgan Hill.*

*Yet 'progress' has not
modernized it quite;
Two well, perchance of
Brigid's day, remain;
A grey church holds the
ancient Celtic site,
By Cromwell's school-
house, solid, grim and plain'.*

The two roads which link Stillorgan with the village of Dundrum date back to the 16th century. The Lower Kilmacud Road via Goatstown is the oldest of the two, and dates to at least 1760, while the Upper Kilmacud Road dates to about 1779.

There are few traces left today of the old Stillorgan village. The original settlement of the village grew up around a number of large estates, mainly along the main road to Bray. In the early days of its development, the street of slated houses referred to by Dalton, commenced with Baumann's store. This street extended to the junction with Kilmacud Road, and continued to Licken's Boot and Shoe repair shop, at the bottom of the hill. On the opposite side of the length of this street was a high wall which belonged to the local estate. The main street on the Kilmacud Road from the junction was also built on one side of the street with the wall of *'Glen Albyn'*. This early development of the village accounts for the origin of the phrase *"all to one side, like Stillorgan"*.

The oldest establishment of the village community is *'Bolands Pub',* the ownership of which can be traced back through the same family lines to the 19th century. A Boland proprietor married into the previous Cullen family, which were the owners of the land since 1764. In the early 1900s, Mrs Boland ran these premises which included a grocery department. This establishment was frequented in the 1940s by Myles na gCopaleen, Jack Doyle and Brendan Behan. It was sold in July 1985.

Other long running family businesses have unfortunately closed in the last few years as traditional crafts and services have declined. One example of such craft that is slowly vanishing is that of shoe repair and manufacture, a craft that formed its own guild in 1427, and at the turn of the last century there were four such shops in the village. One was Licken's Boot and Shoe repair shop. Established in 1917 by Paddy Licken, his son Sean closed its doors for the last time in 1998.

Some shoemakers develop a specialty for working with either lady's or men's shoes, but according to Paddy Licken... *"A good craftsman, no matter how heavy the material you'd give him, he'd have it lightened down into a fine piece, made really into a fine shoe"*.

The following is part of a reflection which Sean Licken, and many of his co-craft workers displayed in their shops…

"A Reminder…
That the soles of the People we keep in view,
For we are the Doctors of the Boot and Shoes,
We sole the living, but not the Dead,
With the best of leather, wax and thread.
We sow on a sole, or nail it fast,
Do a good job and make it last".

The stately home of *'Mount Eagle'*, later known as Stillorgan Castle, was built on the site of the old Wolverston house. This 18th century three-storey house with its mock battlements was once the residence of the Hon. Chichester Skeffington, MP for Antrim, who became 4th Earl of Massareene, and later by the Dublin banker, Arthur Lee Guinness.

The arrival of the Hospitaller Order of St. John of God at Stillorgan had a checkered beginning. The castle, with its thirty acres of land, was purchased from David Sherlock, Sergeant-at-Law and MP, for the sum of £4,000, plus an annual rent of £160 by the Brothers from the French Province of the Order of St. John of God in June 1882.

The intention of the Order was that this establishment be later converted to a private psychiatric hospital. The fire of 1908 delayed the development plans for a hospital. It was opened initially as a nursing home. The brochure drawn up for the first convalescent residents stated that elderly gentlemen in good health seeking a quiet life were accepted. Drunkenness, contagious diseases, insanity, and epilepsy were not accepted initially. Accommodation and charges were graded, fees being one guinea, £1 10s and £2 per week. The sick paid a little more, at the rate of £2 to £3 per week. The Prior at the time, Bro. Picard, in his correspondence with his superiors in France mentioned that, *"The Irish expect much and pay little"*.

The Order's first prospectus listed the amenities which were provided: included were the spacious grounds with the views of the sea and the mountains, daily Mass in the chapel for the convenience of those gentlemen who spend the morning in town and return by the one o'clock trains to Blackrock or Stillorgan rail stations.

Stillorgan Castle

The slogan *"as safe as Ben Burton"* was frequently quoted in the first thirty years of the 18th century to imply undoubted solvency and unquestionable stability and security. In conjunction with Francis Harrison, Ben set up, what was to become a bank of high reputation. Its services were used by the Government as well as the most influential clientele of the day such as the Duke of Ormonde.

The reputation as an eminent banker earned by Ben Burton was short-lived. On Harrison's death in 1725, Ben took his eldest son Samuel as a partner in the bank. Other partners followed, as did the downfall of the bank. Further damage was done to the name of Burton when various Acts were passed (1733-57) by the Legislature, conferring powers on the Trustees to sell the estates owned by the partners to repay the creditors. The expression *"as safe as Ben Burton"* became employed sarcastically in the years that followed when it was meant to convey insecurity and instability.

Burton Hall, built by Samuel Burton in 1730, had all the characteristics of a Georgian stately residence including panelled rosewood doors and window castings with decorated ceilings. During the occupancy of Henry Guinness (1858), cousin of the brewing family and founder of Guinness Mahon Bank, certain changes were made: the entrance was changed to its present position, large servant's quarters were added as well as the verandah.

The Fitzherbert family took over occupancy and later sold it to Mrs Agnes Ryan in 1927. In 1953 Colonel Hume Dugeon set up residency with his well-known Riding Academy until the mid 1960s. After ten years it lay vacant until it was purchased in 1974 by the then Eastern Health Board, which designated it as a resocialisation unit and Day Care centre. This has been administered to the present day by the Hospitaller Order of St. John of God.

Burton Hall

Olivia Hayes

"Happiness is no laughing matter"

"Lose an hour in the morning, and you will spend all day looking for it".

"to know your ruling passion, examine your castles in the air".

"Honesty is the best policy; but he who is governed by the maxim is not an honest man".

These are examples from a collection of well-known quotes from a former parishioner of St. Brigid's parish – Richard Whately, who later became Archbishop of Dublin,1831-1863. His daughter Blanch was buried at St. Brigid's.

The Church was first mentioned in 1216. This was at a time when Raymond de Carew, a Norman knight, was named as the 'owner' of Stillorgan. Following the dissolution of the monasteries, it fell into disuse and disrepair. The church fields were then rented out to various people, including Jacques Wingfield and the Wolverstons who resided nearby at Stillorgan Castle.

John D'Alton, gives a description of St. Brigid's (1838) in the following lines… *"The church is roomy and in good repair. It has no monumental decorations, but in the churchyard are tombs for the Darleys of Stillorgan, the Goffs, Leslies, Georges of Thornhill, Cornwalls; others to Robert Vance, who died in 1810; the Rev. Edward Beaty, vicar of the parish died in 1818, Eleanor, wife of John Malam of the County of Norfolk…"*

There are two churches dedicated to St. Brigid in south County Dublin - at Stillorgan and Tully. St. Brigid was the patron Saint of Leinster: she entered the convent in Meath when she was fourteen years old, and then went on to found four monasteries. The early church at Stillorgan has a holy well, which is adjacent to Holfields on the Merville Road. With the rebuilding of the church in the early 18th century by Archbishop King and John Allen, many of the former graves unfortunately disappeared.

St. Brigid's Church

Olivia Hayes

Leprosy was quite a common disease in Medieval Dublin where three leper hospitals were established. The setting up of a Leper Colony at Ballygregan soon resulted with its placename being changed by local residents to Leoperstown (Baile na Lobher), town of the Lepers. The name Leoperstown seems to have stuck, and its usage in the parish records continued until the middle of the 19th century. It was initially through corruption and mispronunciation that it eventually became known as Leopardstown.

Leopardstown Park House was built in 1796 by Colonel Charles Henry Coote, M.P. for Maryborough (Portlaoise). The house, two-storeys-over-basement and five windows wide, was constructed in Portland stone. During his lifetime at this residence Colonel Coote, later created Lord on the death of a relative, turned the house and grounds into one of the most beautiful and desirable residences in south County Dublin. The following description from Bonnie Flanagan's book (entitled Stately Homes around Stillorgan) will illustrate the point…

"Leopardstown was considered one of the most beautiful estates in County Dublin, and there was a farm which produced sheep of the "real Wicklow breed" and a garden whose fruit and vegetables were noted for their excellence. It is said that they were used for George IV while he lay in his yacht in Kingstown Harbour (now Dun Laoghaire)".

As a result of the death of Lord Coote, his nephew Eyre Coote resided at the house for some time until he sold it in the 1830s for £7,200 to Fenton Hort. Other families to occupy this residence included Mrs Malcolmson followed by her daughter Mrs Usher.

The next person to make an impression on Leopardstown Park House was James Talbot Power of the whiskey distilling family. Shortly after his purchase of this residence (in 1877), James T Power married Gertrude Frances Hayes. They soon set about the restoration of the house and demesne to its original place of beauty and liveliness. While Gertrude was on holiday in England, James died at Leopardstown in July 1916, and subsequently, Gertrude set up a trust with herself and three trustees for the establishment of a hospital, known initally as 'Hayes's Home for Wounded Soldiers' and later as Leopardstown Park Hospital which now cares for the elderly.

Leopardstown Park Hospital

The earliest settlers have remembered their ancestors by various means through the ages. The first farmers to our island built those huge prehistoric or Megalithic tombs as they are known. These took various forms at different periods in history. Passage tombs seem to predominate the south-west part of the county like those at Tallaght, Saggart and Kingston. These take their names from the stone passage that provides access to a burial chamber within a large mound. While the portal type of tombs seem to occupy sites on the south-east part of the county like those at Brennanstown and Kilternan. These are recognised by their two upright stones which form a portal or entrance to the tomb chamber. The wedge tombs are later and are situated more to the east such as Kilmashogue and Shankhill.

With the Bronze Age, man ceased to build those important tombs for their dead but it is thought that Hillforts may have commenced at this period in history. With the Bronze Age came a change in burial rites. A range of specially designed pottery became associated with burial rites. Some of these burials were covered with stone cairns similar to the site on the Great Sugar Loaf. In other cases, stone lined graves were used like at Edmonstown near Rathfarnham.

The Vikings, possibly best known for the destruction carried out on churches, did in time convert to Christianity. The distinctive grave slabs associated with the Vikings are only to be found in south County Dublin, in the vicinity of Rathdown. These became known as the Rathdown slabs which are recognised by their distinctive type of decoration. Each slab is unique with certain decorations common like herringbone and cupmarks. The designs are based on local Viking art styles. They are found at such church sites as Kilgobbin, Killegar, Kilternan, Tully, Rathfarnham, Rathmichael and Whitechurch.

Rathdown Slabs

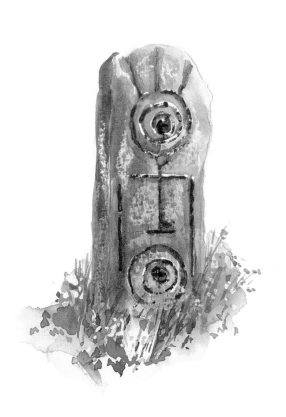

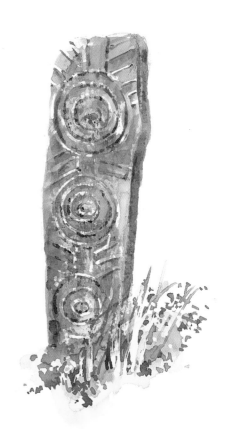

South Dublin, from Vikings to Motorways

1. Viking Era (800-1169)

The Vikings, generally referred to as 'The Danes', were described in Irish folklore as fierce warriors, ravaging the countryside, destroying churches and seizing boys and girls as slaves. It was also claimed that the Vikings imposed a tax of 'an ounce of silver per nose, per year' – those who refused to pay the tax had their nose cut off.

However, as so often with history, before we neatly pigeon-hole these invaders as barbarian destroyers, we should remember that most of the contemporary records of the raids come from the monasteries which were frequently the target of the attacks. It is therefore hardly surprising that these raids and their perpetrators received such bad reports.

Certainly there is other evidence that the fierceness of these Scandanavian raiders engendered a certain respect among their foes. One legend tells how only two Danes survived the battle of Clontarf – a father and son. They were the only two people who knew

the secret recipe which the Vikings had for making beer from heather. The old man was threatened with torture to make him reveal the secret. He agreed but asked that his son be first put to death so that he would not witness his father divulge this secret. This was done but the father then refused, and died under torture rather than reveal the secret.

No matter the feelings of the local people, by the middle of 9th century the Vikings had established a settlement in the vicinity of the area known today as Wood Quay, on the south side of the river Liffey where it is joined by the river Poddle. The *'Annals of Ulster'* tell us of the 'longphort', which was a semi-permanent encampment devised by the Vikings for their plundering and piratical activities. It was also a commercial centre for the sale of slaves and goods during this initial sixty year period of invasion in the years 841-902.

The *'Annals of Ulster'* go on to tell us of the bloody

end of this first Viking venture to the Dublin area when:–

"The heathens were driven from Ireland, … from the fortress [longphort] of Atha Cliath … and they abandoned a good number of their ships, and escaped half dead after they had been wounded and broken."

Thus was Dublin abandoned by these early pillaging invaders who fled to the Isle of Man, the Wirral peninsula and Cumbria.

However any respite was short-lived, for by 917 the invaders were back again. On this occasion they returned to a new south-side location, close to the site of the original settlement overlooking the two same rivers, with the firm intention of founding a trading town overlooking the ford or the *átha cliath* (the name applied to this area in the 6th and 7th centuries).

This time they were more successful, illustrated by evidence of intermingling of the Viking and local cultures around this time. It is recorded that Dublin's first Bishop, Donat, was consecrated in 1028, the same year on which Sitric (son of Óláf) made a pilgrimage to Rome. According to Miles V. Ronan in *'Reportorium Novum'* (1955), this was the Sitric who founded Christ Church (1038) near the original settlement, and whose son, also Sitric, was credited with the foundation of Balally one of the most ancient christian sites around Dundrum.

The original name was Balemicamlaib, i.e. Baile-Mic-Amhlaibh or the town of Óláf, (Auliffe or Olave), indicating a Norse ownership prior to the Anglo-Norman invasion. This Norse influence has echoes right down to the present day in the incorporation of Óláf in the names of a number of clubs in the area.

This was also the period of the commencement of church development into dioceses which began with the Synod of Rath Breasail in 1111, later ratified by the Synod of Kells. With this development of Christianity, the seeds of many of the parishes, towns and villages we see today were sown.

2. THE NORMANS (1169-1315)

The Norman arrival in Ireland was at the invitation of Dermot Mac Murrough who, in the course of a protracted dispute with other Gaelic chieftans, sought assistance from the Anglo-Norman King Henry II – but Dermot got more than he bargained for. The landing of the Normans in May 1169, with their flat ships on the rocky headland known as Baginbun near Bannow Bay in County Wexford, would radically change the course of Irish history.

The Irish defenders with their axes and short swords were no match for these seasoned warriors with their long swords, lances and iron helmets. Unlike the Norse, who mainly inhabited the coast, the Norman occupation spread throughout the country. During the first decades of their arrival, they lived in motte-and-bailey structures which were later replaced by stone castles or tower houses. Their occupation was to have far-reaching effects for the entire country in areas of strategic defence, a system of central administration, fostering of culture, development of an agricultural plan and such like projects.

Soon after their landing in Wexford the Normans moved north to take over the settlements in Dublin and fortifications were soon established throughout the area. As the conquest progressed, ownership of lands previously under the rule of Gaelic Chieftains was taken over by the incoming Norman lords. One of the earliest examples of this in the Dundrum area was the granting of land to the Anglo-Norman family of de Clahull: ownership followed through the family line including Sir John, and later Sir Hugh de Clahull, and then his son-in-law, Sir Walter Purcell.

In an interesting aside, it was around this time that the first reference to the placename Taney – the ancient name for Dundrum – is to be found in the Charter of St. Laurence O'Toole to Christchurch in

1178 as *"half of Rathnahi"*, and again on the following year, in a Bull of Alexander III to the same Archbishop as *"Medietatem de Tignai"*. The variants in the spelling of this placename continue through the following four centuries until the mid 1500s when the name is clarified to mean the church of Taney as the church of 'Nathi' who was the founder and patron saint of this church in Dundrum. The feast day was set aside as August 9th. Little is known about St. Nahi except that in his '*Lives of the Saints*', Butler describes him in the following manner… *"St Nathy Cruimthir, that is, the priest, was a native of the Luighne district of Sligo and is mentioned in the life of St. Attracta, who was probably his contemporary. He is said to have been put to Achonry by St. Finnian of Clonard, though the name by which he was known makes it unlikely that he was a bishop. No biography either in Latin or in Irish seems to be available"*.

But back to the Normans. Wherever they settled, a motte, a manor, or a castle was established, then a mill followed by houses for the officers and retainers: markets were held and eventually towns were developed – often enclosed by walls, such as at New Ross and Drogheda.

The results of excavations carried out at the castle at Dundrum tell some of the story of what life was like in the locality for the new landlords at the end of the 13th and into the 14th century. The dig was directed by Elizabeth O'Brien in 1989, and recovered large quantities of green glazed pottery known as 'Leinster Ware', unglazed cooking ware, some shards of pottery from Saintonge in France, quantities of oyster and cockle shells, and the bones of butchered animals. This indicates that the 13th-14th century occupants of the castle used local pottery, ate shellfish and meat, and drank French wine. A more thorough examination of samples of fill taken from the moat will throw further light on their way of life.

Perhaps more important than their forts and castles, the Normans passed on a culture to the Irish that is ever present. Irish history of this period is taught to the present day generation of school children both in a superior quality and in a more meaningful manner than was perhaps the case in days gone by. Today's students understand that the Anglo-Normans were in fact a multi-ethnic group with French, Dutch, English and Welsh backgrounds. The contribution of this Norman civilisation is illustrated by the research of Paul Cotter ('*Irish Roots*', 1997), with his examples of this multi-ethnic influence within the language we use in our society e.g. those words which seem very Irish, like *seomra* (a room), and *garsún* (a boy after being Anglicised as 'gorsoon') derived from French originals – chambre and garçon. In the same way many Christian names which also seem to be Irish today were first borrowed from the Anglo-Normans like

Seán (from Jean), Eamon (from Edmond), Séamus (from James), Piaras/Pierce (from Piers), Siobhán (from Jean). Irish surnames have been influenced in a similar manner by our multi-ethnic origins.

However, no matter what echoes their presence would leave in the future, their arrival in the south Dublin area in the 12th century meant major changes for the people already living there.

The Normans had a keen eye for good agricultural land and large chunks of Dublin's hinterland were retained by them including such places south of the Liffey as Newcastle, Esker, Crumlin and Saggart. This occupation did not necessarily mean the expulsion of the ordinary Irishman from the land. They were needed to herd the cattle and sheep as well as till the land just like they had been doing under their native chieftains. Indeed many may have regarded the arrival of the Normans as a blessing since, once they occupied a locality, peace often seemed to be an outcome where previously there had been raids and counter-raids amongst the Irish clans. For the first time, Ireland was introduced to estate management and systematic agriculture. The development of a parochial system, villages and towns became a reality.

The establishment of these Norman towns was not too well received by the Gaelic chiefs who were the main losers as the new Anglo-Norman settlers pushed them off their old lands. Two families who suffered much in this process were the O'Tooles and the O'Byrnes.

The O'Tooles and the O'Byrnes were originally of the same family line and inhabited those areas now called Kildare. With the Norman invasion they were driven out into that mountainous part of Dublin and north Wicklow referred to as O'Brynes Country. Thus ensued almost three centuries of severe and frequent incursions by these warring families as they launched severe attacks on the farmers of Kilgobbin where the lands of the local residents were plundered and burned. Fiach Mac Hugh O'Byrne was their last chief and died in 1597. The genealogy, and activities of these families are well documented, and illustrated by Rev. P. L. O'Toole, in his *History of the Clan O'Toole*.

Colonisation of the land by Norman lords began to take hold while these warring families continued to wage their raids. Francis E. Ball referred to this with incidences in his book, *A History of the County Dublin*, when he explains, *"being a valued servant of the Crown"*, John de Walhope was rewarded (1279) with the lands of Balally, which were later in the hands of Maurice Howell and Gregory Taunton *"as tenants to the Priory of the Holy Trinity (1334) for the lands of Balally until 1407 when a grant from the Crown was made to William Walsh"*. The result of these skirmishes meant that the ancient church of Balally fell into ruins as apparently the ancient Norse settlement was wiped out; more suitable sites were found for churches of the Irish.

The early stages of the 14th century were a rather turbulent time in history. It was also a period of an attempt at Gaelic revival. Many of the native Irish were working those lands they once owned, now in the hands of Normans – many of whom were referred to as 'absentee landlords' due to their frequent absences from the country. As such it was rather difficult to enforce the rule of law and the tendency for revolt was ever present.

Then there was the invasion of Edward Bruce in 1315. This resulted with devastation of the lands at Farranboley which was part of the Milltown manor, and adjoining the lands of Dundrum. Utter lawlessness prevailed including frequent incursions and assaults on the local residents by the displaced Gaelic landlords. As a result of this unrest the church lands were loosing profits and the archbishop of Dublin was forced to lease these lands as well as those of nearby Churchtown and Taney to such free tenants and retainers as Edmund Hacket, Richard Chamberlain and John Locumbe.

Thus during the first decade of the of the 1300s,

the lands of Kilgobbin passed into the hands of the Hacket family. Shortly afterwards, a branch of the Walshe family from nearby Carrickmines shared these lands on which they built a castle, the ruins of which are to be seen in the village of Kilgobbin. The castle, town and lands were temporarily seized from John Walshe (who died in 1578), but the castle and lands were soon reclaimed and the Walshe family line remained on until the 1690s when the lands and castle came into the hands of the Fitzwilliam family, who already had amassed considerable property and lands in this part of south County Dublin.

3. THE ENGLISH PALE (1400-1500)

After the first waves of the Anglo-Norman Invasion had subsided, the new settlers set about establishing themselves in Dublin. One of the Normans' first priorities was security and they set about clearing any natives who had not sworn allegiance to the Crown from the countryside immediately outside the settlement. This allowed the settlers to carry on with their agriculture, which was their main food source, without fear of attack. To further secure the area, this English land (or the 'Pale' as it became known) was then enclosed by what has been known as the 'Pale Ditch'. This enclosure was supported on the outside by a chain of defensive tower houses and castles such as at Rathfarnham, Dundrum and Carrickmines.

By the the early 15th century the entire complexion of the Norman presence in Ireland had radically changed. Most of the settlers had either been driven out by the original Gaelic families or (in many cases) had been assimilated through marriage into the native population. As such, the Norman occupation of Ireland could be considered to be at an end – except for the Pale.

The land within the Pale was still entirely under the control of the English settlers, and surrounding this was a type of buffer zone known as the 'march' or boundary. This boundary stretched from Dalkey to Merrion, and on to Saggart including Rathcoole, Kilkeel, Rathmore, Ballymore-Eustace, Naas, Clane, and to Dundalk. This was the extent of the Pale in 1488 when it included most of the four counties of Kildare, Meath, Louth and Dublin. Various attempts were made to reinforce this defence like the 1494 Act of Parliament, (known as Poynings' Law) which required landowners to construct a new line of defence along the borders of the Pale. This was to take the form of a double ditch of almost two metres high above the ground on one side. The rationale behind this attempt was to cause a hindrance to movement. The principal source of wealth at the time was cattle, and so the Pale ditch was a deterrent to obstruct the theft of cattle from within the Pale. In the law he enacted, Sir Edward Poynings stated that *"As the marches of the four shires lie open and not fensible in fastness of ditches and castles, by which*

Irishmen do get hurt in preying the same; it is enacted that every inhabitant, each tiller, and occupier of the said marches - i.e. in the County of Dublin, Kildare, Meath, and Uriel [Louth]…".

This link between landowning and contributing to defence can also be seen in action in 1539 when King Henry VIII presented the lands of Balally to the Corporation of Dublin, which in turn leased them to Jacques Winfield, Master of the King's Ordnance on condition that he build a castle on the site. The castle was never completed because of the hostile incursions of the Wicklow clans. The castle outline could be traced within living memory at the rear of Balally Terrace. The memory of the ancient church remained, and it is fitting that the two parties – politics and family feuds forgotten – agreed to build the Cross Church of Moreen in 1815.

In the 1580s Rathfarnham Castle was built as a stately home by Archbishop Adam Loftus who wrote twenty years later about the damage inflicted by the frequent raids of those two families from the mountains. He wrote:– *"This common calamity hath now light heavely upon myself for even at the writing hereof, the rebels of these mountains by Dublin watching an opportunity to have attempted something against my house at Rathfarnham have not let so much as one beef, or mutton to feed my family".*

Rob Goodbody, in his book entitled *'On the Borders of the Pale'* (1993), carried out considerable research as to the extent of evidence of what remains of this Pale ditch. He discovered some remains of a well-preserved section of this ditch of the Pale at Ballyogan and again between Carrickmines and Kilgobbin both of which had castles which were owned by the Walshe family at the time the ditch was constructed. According to Rob Goodbody it was only local tradition that kept alive the memory of the Pale ditch in the area of Kilcross (presently a private housing area in the vicinity of Balally) long after it was forgotten in history.

4. THE REBELLION (1600s)

By the early 17th century the power struggle between the English parliament and King Charles I was being viewed with increasing alarm by catholics, both Irish and English, living in Ireland. Should the strongly puritan parliament gain the upper hand, there was every reason to believe that their policy would be to suppress the catholic worship which Charles had permitted. At the same time some of the old Gaelic landlords saw the turmoil in England as an opportunity to regain their old position and in 1641 open rebellion began in Ulster.

In south County Dublin there had been an uninterrupted presence of a long line of English catholic landlord families who were sympathetic to their catholic subjects and it was considered prestigious for a landlord to keep a friar or priest on their premises. The Walshes and the Fitzwilliams are examples of such families who were known to have kept a priest to celebrate Mass for the local community.

However not all the landlords in the Dundrum area shared the same views. The neighbouring Loftus family were greatly concerned that their base at Rathfarnham would be under threat. Every precaution was taken to prevent the castle falling into the hands of the rebels on the outbreak of the Rebellion of 1641 and all the Loftus family took up arms. Various outrages were committed in the immediate neighbourhood of the castle and, in various skirmishes, considerable damage was done as a result of the use of gunpowder.

The outcome was that the castle lay derelict for a number of years until its restoration. The castle at Rathfarnham was later acknowledged by Francis E. Ball as one of the finest in County Dublin. The ownership passed in direct family line of descent from Adam Loftus until 1726, when the then owner, the Duke of Wharton, had to sell the estate to defray his debts. The Loftus family line returned to Rathfarnham castle in the late 1700s when the castle became renowned for the luxury of its famed collections of art, gardens and aviaries. By the end of

the century the castle was described as abandoned with its art collection dispersed to other Loftus residences. By the mid 1800s the castle, described as being in a ruinous state, was purchased by the Lord Chancellor Blackburne who was responsible for its modernisation. The castle was declared a National Monument in 1986 and was purchased for the Nation in the following year.

The most eminent catholic landlord in south County Dublin at this time was Oliver Fitzwilliam. Initially a firm Royalist, in the early 1640s he raised an army of 3,000 men in Ireland before the Rebellion for service in France. Although this army was never brought to conflict, Oliver continued to press for the acceptance of Catholic demands regarding their religious beliefs. The complete triumph of Cromwell and the puritans in England (and subsequently in Ireland) meant huge losses for the Fitzwilliam dynasty. Their estates and lands in Kilternan were confiscated with all their other possessions.

Fortunately for Oliver, his luck changed with his second marriage to Eleanor Holles, daughter of the first Earl of Clare. Her family were committed supporters of parliament and were able to intervene to save Oliver from the full fury of the victors. This led to Oliver's eventual and productive friendship with Cromwell.

After Cromwell's death in 1660 and the restoration of the monarchy one might have thought that Oliver's 'flexibility' would catch up with him. However once again Oliver's luck held and Charles II, mindful of his long and loyal service, fully restored Oliver Fitzwilliam. He was also created Earl of Tyrconnell in 1663. In a grant to Oliver, the Second Viscount of Fitzwilliam, Charles II, (1666) confirmed to him the lands of Dundrum, Ballinteer, Ticknock, Merrion, Baggotrath (Baggot Street), Donnybrook (the mill only), Kilmacud, Booterstown, Glencullen and other lands.

In later years, Mary Fitzwilliam married Henry, Earl of Pembroke in 1733, and so began the Pembroke dynasty that was to share and administer the Fitzwilliam lands. Pembroke later became a township (1863) and by the end of the century the Earl of Pembroke was responsible for the construction of those Pembroke cottages for his estate workers at Irishtown and the village of Dundrum. Oliver died in April 1667, and the Fitzwilliam lands were passed on through the family line until 1833 when John, the Eighth and last Viscount of Merrion died. This was the end of a three century line of the Fitzwilliam stronghold.

Kilgobbin, in the late 17th century was of sufficient status to be known as a town. Townlands like this were frequently referred to in deeds as 'the town and lands of…'. Given that there were no industries at Kilgobbin, the residents lived on produce from the land. On the occasion of a Regal visitation in 1615, the church was found to be in ruin, and this was the case until 1707, when Archbishop King had the ruins removed, and a Protestant church erected on the site which continued until 1826. The ruins of this latter mentioned church were on an elevated plateau, and towered over the cemetery that contained the remains of such families as the Taylors of Harold's Grange, the Deakens, the Millikins, the Harknesses, the Davies, and the Hutchinsons. Many of these burials date back to the 1720s.

5. THE 18TH CENTURY

Through the 1700s, village activities in Dundrum centred on the castle itself. Colonel Isaac Dobson undertook restoration of the buildings, added an artificial lake and set out the gardens. Alderman Eliphal Dobson succeeded the ownership of the castle on the death of his father in 1700. Eliphal continued the development of the gardens. This is described in the August 1897 edition of *'The Irish Builder'* by Francis E. Ball as follows – *"with neatly cut yew trees, while behind it a grove of ash trees stretched down to the river, and adjacent to it lay a pretty pleasure-ground and kitchen garden".* It seems from this report that he was an affluent resident of Dundrum. He could afford such luxuries as well as furnished houses, books, horses and carriages. No doubt, one of the sights of Dundrum was to see the worthy Alderman proceeding in his great heavy coach to and from the castle. On his death in March 1720 he was buried in St. Werburgh's Church on St. Patrick's Day.

Towards the end of the 18th century, considerable interest and effort were devoted to gardens and gardening in the 'Big Houses' (or Seats as they were referred to) of Ballinteer. Besides suggestions as to how gardens should be kept, detailed descriptions are also given together with some criticisms of local gardens. These have been referred to individually by Archer who concludes with the reference "*There are thousands of small neat houses, elegant demesnes with good gardens … not to be surpassed, either for number or elegance.*" This interest in gardens has also been borne out by the considerable number of gardeners who resided within the townland, as indicated in records of the occupations of the adults recorded in the 1901 and 1911 census. Also at this period, the townland of Ballinteer and its surrounding townlands were emerging from what might be called its prairie condition, farms were gradually being changed into well-kept places surrounded by high walls and trees.

18th century literature describes the lands in the southern townlands of Dundrum as used extensively for forestry. The plantation and the growing of trees was considered a worthwhile investment. This was the raw material for shipbuilding and commerce. Detailed records of tree growing such as the 'Registry of Trees', kept by the Clerk of the Peace, were maintained. According to an 1765 Act, a financial incentive was given to residents who planted such specific varieties of trees such as ash, elm, sycamore, oak and beech. These records, described by Joseph Archer, in his book entitled '*Statistical Survey of the County of Dublin*' (1801), illustrate the point that the environs of Dundrum were key areas for supplying such vital raw material.

Richard Johnston and Valentine Dunn planted a total of 10,596 trees in Ballinteer, while in the local townland of Balally, James Towers planted some 909. Later records indicate that Richard Johnston of Ballinteer had these trees registered with the Clerk of the Peace for the County Dublin on April 4th 1801. From these records, it may be noted that he had planted a considerable quantity and variety including: beech, larch, birch, lime, oak, silver fir, silver poplar and sycamore. Archer, in his extensive observations of the countryside made references to the poor state of woodlands in the County of Dublin, and the price of timber. He went on to make some strong recommendations for long term investments in forestry as a resource for the future.

Various suggestions were also given as to how best to grow the different varieties of trees.

Amongst his observations on one of his three tours of Ireland, towards the end of the 1700s, Arthur Young, a travelling historian (d.1820) made certain statements regarding the denudation of the countryside of this valuable resource and the general state of 'timber and plantations'. He referred to a number of areas when he said that the localities *"exhibit a naked, bleak, dreary view for want of wood which has been destroyed"*. He then goes on to state that this destruction *"was due to the common people who steal it for a walking stick and afterwards for a spade handle and later a car shaft and later still for a cabin rafter"*.

He observed that the poor were not entirely at fault when he referred to the fact that *"the profligate, prodigal, worthless landowner cuts down his acres and leaves them unfenced against cattle, and then he has the impudence to charge the scarcity of trees to the walking sticks of the poor"*.

When we read these observations of Archer we are reminded of the words of *Cill Chais*, a poem written by the unknown 17th century poet (*Ón mBealoideas* – 'word of mouth'), still sung today in Gaelic,

"Cad a dhéanfaimid feasta gan adhmad?
Tá deireadh na gcoillte ar lár;
Níl trácht ar Chill Chais ná a teaghlach,
'S ní cluinfear a cling go brách -
An áit úd 'na gcónáiodh an dea-bhean
Fuair gradam is meidhir thar mhná,
Bhíodh iarlaí ag tarraingt thar toinn ann
Is an tAirfreann binn dá rá".

And its English translation…

What shall we do without timber
Now that the forests are all cut down?
It shall never be surpassed,
There is no talk of Kilcash,
where the good woman lived,
Praised and respected beyond all others
Earls came there from abroad
And melodious Mass was there celebrated.

6. 19TH CENTURY

Having been largely by-passed by the events of the United Irishmen uprising in 1798, in the early decades of the 1800s Dundrum and the surrounding areas were well-known for the therapeutic nature of their location as illustrated by the following quote from Brewer, in his *'Beauties of Ireland'* who described Taney as *"in this rural hamlet are many romantic cottages whose white fronts and low proportions would appear to harmonise with the wishes*

People

of those who frequent the place, by holding forth the soothing invitations of retirement and peace".

And again, he refers to the locality as *"Dundrum is in a sheltered declivity, sheltered from the harsh winds. The village is in the fashionable resort of invalids for the purpose of drinking goat's whey. At early hours of the morning numerous jaunting cars convey from the city large parties of visitors to partake of that sanative beverage amidst the reviving scenery over which the animals have browzed".*

The villages of Rathfarnham, Stillorgan and Dundrum were interconnected, not only by a transport system but also by good quality roads in the early 19th century. There was a regular coach service provided to and from the city of Dublin, with a two-tier fare system in operation for passengers. For the single journey of five miles it cost 1s 3d for the passenger who travelled inside the coach, while it cost 10d for the passenger who chose to be exposed to the elements making this journey on the outside. These charges were considered costly at the time.

The thoroughfare system from Dublin to Enniskerry passed through Dundrum, Sandyford, Kilgobbin and Stepaside. The Ballinteer Road and Stepaside Hill are two roads which are well-known for their antiquity and were linked to Glencullen. According to Rob Goodbody's research, it would

seem that, at the end of the 18th century, there was a boom of new road-building most likely to facilitate the mobilization of troops (an encampment was located at Loughlinstown) in the 1790s in case of a French invasion. The introduction of the mail coaches in the 1780s was a further reason for implementing a road improvement programme and besides, a considerable amount of granite had to be transported from the quarries in the Barnacullia area to various parts of Ireland.

The roads in this southern part of County Dublin which date back to this period include Ballyogan Road, Glenamuck Road, Enniskerry Road, Blackglen Road and Hillcrest Road. These were followed in the 1840s by the Leopardstown Road leading to Sandyford Cross. The connecting section of road to Whites Cross was built at a slightly later date. One of the greatest coups to be achieved by Dundrum in the field of transport was the railway link in 1854. This brought with it economic activity and numerous benefits.

The rail line was extended to Wicklow, Wexford and then to Waterford, allowing Dundrum to interact with these towns. The railway was efficient and, as it was the primary link station between Harcourt Street and Shankhill, Dundrum became a hub of business and social activity. The village also became a popular choice for those seeking a better, more desirable place to live and large villas sprang up on the properties around the area. Those years gave the village the basic shape it holds to the present day.

Conditions of living locally in the last decade of the 1700s and early 1800s for the south side of the Dublin have been described by Joseph Archer in his *'Statistical Survey of the County of Dublin'*. To illustrate the cost of living in what was a rural setting for the environs of Dundrum, we can draw from this work the following examples of prices which varied at certain times of the year i.e. from April to August of 1801 – beef per pound, from10d to 6d; mutton per pound, from 10d to 6d; veal, from 10d to 6d; potatoes per stone, 1s 9d to 9d; herrings per hundred, 6s to 4s 4d while cod could be purchased in the market at 2d per pound; milk from 6d to 4d per quart; butter per pound from 1s 4d to 1s; eggs per hundred from 7s to 6s; bread from 1s for 3lb 8oz in April and for 3lb 11oz in August.

To put these prices into context one needs to look at wages of the time. Labourer's wages for those south Dublin suburbs in 1801 ranged from 8s to 9s per week if engaged in constant employment throughout the year, while the rate for temporary work was 9s 9d per week. There were other criteria for earnings: *"in harvest time, more according to the mode of their employment, whether with or without provisions, the necessity of the time, or other*

contingencies". Other rates of pay were in operation e.g. potatoes were planted by piece work at 3d per perch (six metres in length and three metres broad) for ridge and furrow. While on other occasions there would be an agreed costing for a particular job: turnips are twice hoed for 21s per acre; the rate for digging loose ground was 3d to 3d per square perch; hay was moved from 6s 6d to 10s per acre according to the crop, i.e. whether the hay was lodged or not.

Archer further relates that conditions of employment were clearly laid down as *"The time of labour is fixed for six o'clock in the morning to six in the evening, allowing, out of that time, half an hour for breakfast, and one hour for dinner. In the harvest time they work from sunrise to sunset, and in the winter, as long as they can see".* Farmers and others were encouraged pay their workers at such times and places so as to oblige the men, *"to go for change to the meat shops or bakers, and not to whiskey shops to dissipate their hard earnings".*

The suburbs of Rathfarnham and Dundrum were in relative close proximity to the Dublin mountains and the sources of the rivers Dodder, Dargle, Swan, Slang and others. These rivers were harnessed for mills which provided considerable employment throughout this area of south County Dublin. There was a proliferation of mills in the Dundrum,

Rathfarnham, Milltown, Whitechurch, and Stillorgan localities.

At Dundrum, Mrs Hall had a paper-mill: Mr Stokes operated three mill-wheels as well as an iron works; at Marlay, Rt. Hon. David La Touche operated a threshing-mill; at Milltown, Mr Hunt had two woollen-mills; Messrs Burk and Mullen had three woollen-machines, log-wood, and oil-mills; at Rockbrook, Mr Nun operated six paper-mills; at Donnybrook, Mr Dillon operated four cotton-mills: at Clonskeagh, Jackson and White operated two iron-work wheels while Mr Stokes & Co. operated three of these mills. Rathfarnham accommodated four-mills, and these included a flour-mill operated by Messrs Newman, Curraghan and Flanagan: Mr Freeman and Teeling had a paper-mill each while Mr Dumgold operated a corn-mill. The following places also operated a number of mills: Kimmage (5); Harold's Cross (3); Templeogue (4); Dolphin's Barn (2); Rathmines (2): and Kilternan (1). In contrast, the suburbs on the flat land on the north side of County Dublin were engaged in the development of a different type of employment resources. These included fourteen wind-mills in operation with only one corn-mill and a water-mill.

Having survived as a corn-mill for three hundred years, the last mill at Dundrum was transformed into what was known as the Manor Mill laundry, which was the largest employer of female labour in the district. It was located in the area where the old Dundrum Bowling Complex once stood. By 1943, the mill was taken over by Pye Ireland Ltd., which employed 1,200 males and 650 females in the manufacture of cabinet surrounds for radio and television sets. As a result of changing styles, it was forced to close its doors in 1985.

The occupations of many of the residents of those places on the Dublin mountains such as Sandyford, Barnacullia and Glencullen was initially determined by the geology of the surrounding area. The craft of stone-cutting has been perfected through the generations of particular families to such an extent that the skill has become innate. The names of the quarries that have been worked by individual families through generations are synonomous with those families.

Nicholas Ryan has given some insight into the extent and history of the craft of stone-cutting in the locality of south county Dublin when he wrote in his book entitled *'Sparkling Granite'* (1992)

"The connection with local granite is clearly established from about 1740 by reference to Quarries beyond Kilgobbin which were subject to various improvements and were supplanting the use of Portland stone in building. In the 1770s there

are records of stone from Kilgobbin being used by the Paving Board. A contractor called Arthur Bucton claimed that he had engaged Kilgobbin quarries for a term of years and from there he was bringing stones and flags that none could equal for goodness. So good were they that he was prepared to keep his work in repair for twice as long as any other contractor".

The list of public buildings erected with this granite from the Dublin mountains is extensive, with quarries such as Ballybrew, Glencullen Mountain Quarries, Peter Walshe's Quarry, Pat Donnelly's Quarry at Barnaculia, the Black Quarries, the Blue Light Quarry, and the Turk Doyle's Quarry shipping stone all over Ireland and beyond. Today, four of those quarries continue the craft of stone-cutting.

A reference to the transport of this granite was recorded for the 1935 Folklore collection of UCD by local twelve year old Michael O'Keeffe, while a pupil at Sandyford National School in the following words, *"Before motor lorries were invented, large numbers of men and horses and carts were employed to carry the stone … As well as this, freestone was largely used by housewives in Dundrum, Blackrock and Dun Laoghaire for scrubbing and many people used to go around from door to door selling it".* This stone was used for scrubbing white deal kitchen tables.

7. 20TH CENTURY

The early part of the 20th century village of Dundrum had no less than three royal visits. In 1900, the motorcade of Queen Victoria, in her visit to Dublin, passed through Rosemount to Mount Anville to visit the Dargan family. Then, in July 1907, King Edward and Queen Alexandra attended the races at Leopardstown Racecourse and returned by way of Sandyford and the Village of Dundrum. Five years later, in 1911 King George V and Queen Mary drove in an open carriage on route to visit the Hodgins family who resided at Beaufort, opposite the Loreto Abbey in Rathfarnham. A bronze medallion was issued to commemorate the occasion at a cost of one shilling.

Within four years of the last royal visit to Dublin, the Irish Volunteers set themselves up as an army with the military purpose of ending British rule in Ireland. There were many volunteers to the cause from south Dublin, but perhaps the best known was Countess Markievicz.

Countess Markievicz, née Gore-Booth, born in London, was also involved in this struggle for freedom for south County Dublin. Her interest first became aroused when she rented a house in Balally, and discovered back issues of the publication entitled *'Peasant and Sinn Féin'*, which were left by the previous tenant, Pádraic Colum (poet and dramatist). Her interest in Irish politics developed and in 1908 she joined Sinn Féin.

Besides being responsible for the foundation of *Na Fianna* in 1909, the Countess was involved in the running of a soup kitchen in Liberty Hall during the 1913 lock-out of workers in Dublin. She was assisted with the setting up of Na Fianna by Helena Molony who was also a patriot. Helena was arrested in 1911 during the protests organised by Sinn Féin against the visit of King George V. She too had a part to play in the attack on Dublin Castle in the 1916 Rising, as a result of which she was imprisoned at Aylesbury Jail (Bucks., England), until the end of 1916.

In the 1916 Rising the Countess served at the College of Surgeons, St. Stephen's Green under Michael Mallin (one of the signatories to be executed in Kilmainham Jail), and was condemned to death. Her sentence was commuted to penal servitude for life: she was imprisoned at Aylesbury Jail, and later released in the general amnesty of June 1917. She was then on the run, and later served two jail sentences, in Mountjoy, Dublin and Cork. However she continued to advocate Republican views, was arrested in November 1923 and went on hunger strike. She later joined Fianna Fáil when it was founded by Éamon de Valera. She was buried in the Republican plot at Glasnevin cemetery in July 1927.

During the early post-war era, the southside perimeter of the city maintained a rural atmosphere although many of its formerly private villas and their extensive grounds were now occupied by schools, colleges and hospitals (often run by the religious orders). Even though the area was only 3 miles from the city centre, interspersed amongst these establishments was open countryside much of which was in agricultural use. For anyone visiting the area for the first time today in 2002, it might be difficult to appreciate just how open some localities were, given they are now so firmly established in the main built up area of the suburbs of Dublin.

In the early 1950s rapid changes began to take place throughout those areas in the vicinity of Dundrum. At the Lower Kilmacud Road in Stillorgan, farms and estates were selling off parts of their land to property developers and, by 1951, private family homes had been built at Dale Road and Dale Drive.

On the southern environs of Dundrum village there was Simpson's Hospital (once Wyckham) and to the east side of the village there was Airfield, famous for their Jersey herd. Today, the only representative of those dwelling houses with surrounding farmland is the Airfield Trust estate in Dundrum.

By the 1960s there was a tendency towards the decentralisation of industry and retailing. The first suburban shopping centre was built at Stillorgan in 1966. A total of over sixty such centres have since been built, with Liffey Valley being the largest. The shopping centre at Dundrum was built in the early 1970s on what was then a mink farm.

Concurrent with these developments there was an acute increase in the population. The green fields of Pine Valley, Kingston, Woodpark and such townlands in the parish of Ballinteer of the 1970s are now replaced with private homes. Every effort had to be made to attend to the spiritual, social, educational and physical needs of these families. With reference to attending to the spiritual needs of the population the 1970s was the boom year for the development of parishes and the construction of churches. Prior to 1960 there were 104 parishes in the Catholic Archdiocese of Dublin: today there are 200 parishes. Sixteen of those new parishes are contained within the geographic area of our sojourn and the average size of each of these parishes would range between four and five thousand families. Schools had to be built to accommodate this new population.

Finally, we witness major environmental changes to the areas of Ballinteer, Ticknock and especially the village of Dundrum. The plans for the Southern Cross route, which were first mooted in 1970, are coming to fruition with the construction of Luas and the completion of the M50. Not only will this project create a major contemporary landmark, with the construction of the new suspension bridge, it perhaps signifies in quite a physical way, the final stage of the absorbsion of the area into the City of Dublin.

However, with the diversion of traffic away from their crowded streets, the villages at the gateway to the mountains can perhaps regain some of the feeling of rural calm which has, over the years, made them such attractive retreats from the hustle and bustle of city life.

BIBLIOGRAPHY

Aalen, F.H.A. & Whelan, Kevin (Ed.): *Dublin City and County: from Prehistory to Present,* (1992)

Archer, Joseph: *A Statistical Survey of the County of Dublin,* (1801)

Ball, Francis E.: *A History of County Dublin,* (1902)

Brady, Joseph & Simms, Anngret (Ed.): *Dublin through Space and Time,* (2001)

Corlett, Christiaan: *Antiquities of Old Rathdown,* (2002)

D'Alton John: *The History of the County Dublin,* (1838)

Flanagan, Bonnie: *Stately Homes around Stillorgan,* (1998)

Goodbody, Rob: *On the Borders of the Pale,* (1993)

Ingram, John A.: *The Cure of Souls. A History of St Brigid's, Stillorgan,* (1997)

Nolan, James: *Changing Faces,* (1985)

Joyce, Weston St John: *The Neighbourhood of Dublin,* (1912)

O'Gríofa, Micheál: *Our Lady of the Wayside National School, Kilternan,* (1990)

Pearson, Peter: *Between the Mountains and the Sea,* (1999)

Praeger, Robert Lloyd: *The Way that I Went,* (1937)

Purcell, Mary: *A Time for Sowing,* (1979)

Ronan, Miles V.: *History of the (Dublin) Diocese; Reportorium Novum,* (1955)

Ryan, Christopher (Ed.): *Lewis' Dublin,* (2001)

Ryan, Nicholas M.: *Sparkling Granite,* (1990)

Swords, Kieran: *Ballyroan Townland: delineation and decline,* (2001)

Turner, Kathleen: *If you seek Monuments,* (1983)

Tweed, Carol R.: *Taney, Portrait of a Parish,* (1994)

SOURCES

Three Rock Panorama, Vol. 27, No. 10, November 2001: Vol. 28, No. 3, March 2002

Shannon, Denis, et al. Marlay (1700-2000), Millennium Project, (1998)

The Irish Times, January 6th 2002

Irish Roots, 1997.

Archaeology in County Dublin, Office of Public Works, 1993

Simmington, Robert C., The Civil Survey of County Dublin, (1654-56)

Ball, F.E., The Irish Builder, August 15th 1897; pp. 172-163

Dublin's Victorian Houses, Mary Daly, et al (1998)

Walsh, Thomas F., Favourite Poems we learned in School, As Gaelige, (1994)

AUTHOR ACKNOWLEDGMENTS

I have many people to thank for their assistance and encouragement. My greatest debt is to my family, especially my wife Lily whose time I borrowed during this project.
I also wish to say a special 'Thank You' to the following for their invaluable assistance:

David C. Sheehy, Diocesan Archivist, Archbishop's House, Drumcondra, Dublin 9
Anthony Lynch, Researcher/Teacher, Ballinteer Drive, Dublin 16
Richard Pilkington, Archaeologist, Kilternan, Co. Dublin
Kevin Harrington, Historian, Campfield Terrace, Dundrum, Dublin 14
Kieran Swords, Social Studies Librarian, South Dublin Library, Tallaght, Dublin
John Lennon, Local Historian, Dundrum, Dublin 14

Dear Reader

This book is from our much complimented illustrated book series which includes:-

Belfast	Dundalk & North Louth
By the Lough's North Shore	Drogheda & the Boyne Valley
East Belfast	Blanchardstown, Castleknock and the Park
South Belfast	Dundrum, Stillorgan & Rathfarnham
Antrim, Town & Country	Limerick's Glory
Inishowen	Galway on the Bay
Donegal Highlands	Armagh
Donegal, South of the Gap	Ring of Gullion
Fermanagh	The Mournes
Omagh	Heart of Down
Cookstown	Strangford Shores

For the more athletically minded our illustrated walking book series includes:-

Bernard Davey's Mourne   Tony McAuley's Glens
Bernard Davey's Mourne Part 2

Also available in our 'Illustrated History & Companion' Range are:-

City of Derry   Holywood   Ballymoney
Lisburn   Banbridge

And from our Music series:-

Colum Sands, Between the Earth and the Sky

We can also supply prints, individually signed by the artist, of the paintings featured in the above titles as well as many other areas of Ireland.

For details on these superb publications and to view samples of the paintings they contain, you can visit our web site at **www.cottage-publications.com** or alternatively you can contact us as follows:-

Telephone: +44 (028) 9188 8033   Fax: +44 (028) 9188 8063

Cottage
Publications

**Cottage Publications
is an imprint of
Laurel Cottage Ltd
15 Ballyhay Road
Donaghadee, Co. Down
N. Ireland, BT21 0NG**